I0092652

TRANSFORMATIONAL NURSE IDENTITIES

How to revolutionise your leadership

MICHELLE TAYLOR

B2B

'Michelle Taylor is a health care insider with clinical experience in intensive and emergency care. In her book *Transformational Nurse Identities* Michelle provides nurse leaders with clear models, practical advice and real-life case examples that enable them to be better leaders in today's challenging health leadership context.

'Healthcare leadership has always had its rewards and its challenges but the COVID-19 pandemic has presented unprecedented challenges for nurses and nurse leaders, and the ability to attract, retain and develop nurses is more than ever one of the most critical issues of our time.

'Michelle's book covers a wide range of leadership and emotional intelligence concepts, adding vital tools to the nurse leader's toolkit that enables them to be leaders of transformation of people, culture and patient care.

'I know from numerous nurse leaders that have been lucky enough to participate in Michelle's training that her core messages and strategies resonate with nurse leaders and inspire them to become better leaders. If we are to attract and retain the nursing workforce, this seems like an excellent place to start and a wise investment.'

Linda Betts, Organisational Consultant health sector
www.lindabetts.com.au

'Michelle has written a must-have guide for any healthcare leader who understands that nursing leadership is the backbone of successful healthcare delivery. Her insights and approach can change the game for any healthcare organisation looking to improve quality, service, productivity, and engagement in an industry that always seems under pressure to address a never-ending list of new challenges.'

Andrew Neitlich, Director, Center for Executive Coaching

'Michelle's book's teachings have directly inspired and provided the mentorship I was searching for as a senior nurse previously reluctant to step into nurse leadership.'

Rebecca North, Clinical nurse consultant, Theatre, Royal Darwin Hospital

'I would recommend this book for all nurses in leadership roles. The author, having a nursing background, is insightful to the challenges and demands that all nurses are dealing with on a day-to-day basis. She recommends practical strategies to enhance your leadership and empower your team to ultimately provide a better workplace where the leaders are unleavable! This book is very relevant to my workplace, and reflecting on challenging issues that arise for me in leading a team on shift. The book covered strategies that could be utilised to address and develop both myself and the team. This would be better for the team and the patients we are caring for.'

Maree Monaghan, ICU ANUM

'I have a Master's in Leadership and Management but feel I gained more from two-day Leadership and Coaching sessions with Michelle than the Master's program. I think this is due to Michelle's exceptional knowledge base, the course content, delivery method and the focus on incorporating these skills and knowledge into everyday practice.'

Wendy Rogers, Clinical Nurse Manager, Theatre, Royal Darwin Hospital

First published in 2023 by Michelle Taylor

© Michelle Taylor 2023
The moral rights of the author have been asserted

All rights reserved. Except as permitted under the *Australian Copyright Act 1968* (for example, a fair dealing for the purposes of study, research, criticism or review), no part of this book may be reproduced, stored in a retrieval system, communicated or transmitted in any form or by any means without prior written permission.

All inquiries should be made to the author.

A catalogue entry for this book is available from the National Library of Australia.

ISBN: 978-1-922764-68-3

Book production and text design by Publish Central
Cover design by Pipeline Design

Disclaimer: The material in this publication is of the nature of general comment only, and does not represent professional advice. It is not intended to provide specific guidance for particular circumstances and it should not be relied on as the basis for any decision to take action or not take action on any matter which it covers. Readers should obtain professional advice where appropriate, before making any such decision. To the maximum extent permitted by law, the author and publisher disclaim all responsibility and liability to any person, arising directly or indirectly from any person taking or not taking action based on the information in this publication.

CONTENTS

It's a challenging time in healthcare

Supporting nurse leaders is a high-leverage activity in any healthcare system. But more than ever, healthcare is under-resourced and under-staffed, making leadership feel like a daunting and stressful role. In this book I share strategies that nurse leaders have said make them feel lighter and more hopeful rather than burnt out and wanting to leave. Many hospitals spend time considering their workforces' engagement but turn a blind eye to keeping their leaders engaged and giving them the skills to do their role. Every army needs engaged and skilled generals to lead them to victory, and not incite a mutiny or a rebellion. What is required is a revolution in the way nurses think about leading that involves new perspectives, not just new knowledge.

ABOUT YOU

You picked up this book as you suspect there could be more you can do as a leader for your team. Times are changing, and you know you need to as well. You know this is a critical time in healthcare.

It's time nurses claimed the professional leadership development that other professionals and organisations have enjoyed for years. You want to turn the tide of nurses leaving the unit, to shift the rising feeling of helplessness that threatens to overtake you with some practical strategies. With all the pressures at work, it's hard to understand how to lead. Your team members are tired and combative. This combativeness leads to more stress and increases negative focus.

There may have even been complaints or grumblings about you, while you think you're doing your best under the circumstances. There's tension because you feel your team might be too sensitive. You think you handle situations well despite the pressure, but there's still confusion. The longer it goes on, the more it's eating away your confidence, and you start to second-guess yourself.

You're afraid there may be another complaint. You might not talk to some nurses you don't get along with while juggling workplace issues and keeping patients safe. You may even avoid feedback conversations as you know they will cause drama, and you don't want to risk the relationships. It might even feel like you're pussy-footing around complex discussions.

You're not the only one dealing with these problems.

If this is you, I see you. I work with people just like you. I've *been* you. I wrote this book for those who are struggling with communication and leading a stressed team. You are also in a changing healthcare landscape so your nursing leadership needs to reach a higher level.

The expectations of you at this time can feel outrageous. The world is shifting, becoming more complex and anxiety-provoking, so nurse leaders have to lead teams whose stress level is higher than at any other time in history. After the recent crisis of the COVID-19 pandemic, we know that disruptions are more likely in the future. Nurse leaders I work with describe their work as a war zone, chaos, mayhem and out of control. Nurses know they have to lead with heart and create a community. But how do you operationalise this? The strategies here will help you succeed. Not only will you feel better about yourself as a leader, but your team will also be happier and more likely to stay and contribute in a meaningful way. Most importantly, your patients will be safer.

The intense stress at work creates drama and politics. Nurse leaders must surf these waves and find a path to lead their teams using outstanding interpersonal skills and a vision worth following. Nurses also demand collective leadership. They want to be part of the journey.

Influence and engagement are the keys to retaining staff in these times. Ken Blanchard, a leading business strategist, author and consultant, says, 'The key to successful leadership is influence, not authority.'

ABOUT ME

I bridge three worlds – nursing, psychology and healthcare leadership – bringing a unique way of looking at nurse leadership. As a former critical care nurse, I've worked in the emergency department (ED) and a neonatal intensive care unit (NICU), but primarily I've been in intensive care units. I worked in intensive care in Darwin through both Bali bombings, and I've had the honour of working in remote Aboriginal communities in the Northern Territory, training Aboriginal healthcare workers.

I retrained as a psychologist in 2008. Since then, I've done a range of counselling and training. I've conducted training at all state and federal government levels, in mines and even a casino. In 2019, I circled back to working in intensive care with teams – training them in teamwork, resilience, leadership and giving feedback. I realised this is where I needed to be – using my skills in healthcare.

Back at university, I studied organisational coaching and leadership. I became an executive coach and then studied health leadership coaching. New leaders' lack of nursing support came to my attention in the late '90s. I was on permanent night duty in an ICU. I had three young kids at the time, so night duty was an easy option for me for childcare. I was made a senior and a team leader but floundered with the lack of support. I remember calling a registrar, who was grumpy and unhelpful. I felt alone with clinical issues. You can imagine my stress levels. I didn't want to come to work and ended up with gastritis from the stress.

Looking back, I can see I needed to ask for mentorship, but I didn't. I didn't know what I needed. I was confused, and I thought I lacked something. That I should have known what to do. I thought then that leadership was something you're either born with or not. A part of the issue then is part of the issue now. Nursing doesn't have a culture of personal development, which impacts communication, teamwork, leadership and retention.

TO BE A SUCCESSFUL LEADER ...

To be a good leader, you don't have to be the smartest in the room, but you do have to be the smartest at removing the obstacles in your team's way. Eliminating these obstacles (including your behaviour) is how you get them to work at their best and ensure your patients receive the best and safest care possible. That is how you keep the top performers in your team. I've seen this happen again and again. I've taken others through these steps. I know that if you apply them, you will see remarkable changes occur too, in any hospital system.

To be a successful leader and be unleavable, you have to take an inside-out perspective. You need to be the person who can help your team members get the clinical results. Transform your relationship with your team by reducing the dramas (the ones you can control) and knowing what needs to happen to retain your team. The good news is you don't sacrifice excellent nursing care or lose yourself. You will gain confidence and passion as you focus on what builds capacity in both you and them. And research shows it preserves your energy, reducing the risk of burnout.

It's essential to protect my clients' privacy, but I also know it's important to share stories from my experience to illustrate points. In some instances, I've changed names and other identifying factors. Others have kindly permitted me to share their stories.

Leading the way in chaotic times needs a practical guide to shift from theory to practice. Nurses are practical, and they also like evidence-based practice. Reading and applying what I outline in this book is your opportunity to get in on the action of leadership development that most nurses don't get. You can be a part of the revolution that leads the evolution of nursing and discards outdated leadership models that you intuitively know don't work anymore. You will learn about the leader you need to be for these times and what your team wants to perform well.

Your emotional intelligence will improve as you learn how to read yourself better and know what to do when your team is stressed. You will discover the common obstacles and triggers that make you leavable and learn how to plan to be better than you have been. Your team becomes followers, and then leaders. I will share information that, up until now, has been only for my nursing leadership mastermind. I will also reveal the simple ways to implement transformational leadership habits using nursing identities and my reflective process that leaves you evolving not only as a nurse leader but as a person, and more hopeful and lighter in what has been an unprecedented dark and heavy time in healthcare.

Michelle Taylor
October 2022

1

The hidden costs of stress

THE LINGERING EFFECTS OF COVID-19 ON HEALTHCARE

The personal toll of the COVID-19 pandemic on hospital staff members will linger for years. Junior nurses (one or two years out of study) are the worst affected. The more inexperienced and younger the healthcare worker at the frontline, the higher the risk to their mental health.[1] The nurses you lead have had this traumatic experience of a global pandemic.

That is why you must change how you lead your clinical team. And it's one reason I have written this book.

An Australian study paints a grim snapshot of the mental health of healthcare workers. Research shows anxiety symptoms at 59.8%, depression at 57.8%, and emotional exhaustion, which points towards burnout, at 70.9%.[2] Another study at a Melbourne hospital in 2020 showed that 29.5% of participants screened

---

1   According to an Australian study by Smallwood et al. (2021) into the second wave of the pandemic.

2   Research by Natasha Smallwood and Karen Willis.

positive for burnout.[3] Rates of depression, anxiety and post-traumatic stress disorder were four to five times the general community's levels. When conducting training in hospitals, I've seen that nurse leaders who have borne the brunt of the pandemic's patients in 2022 most closely identify with burnout and a residual anxiety that doesn't seem to abate.

Mental health is a complex issue. So, I will refer to anxiety, depression, PTSD and burnout symptoms using a single term: stress. As a psychologist, I understand the risks of possibly downplaying the impact of nurses' experiences by categorising these problems as 'stress'. All these conditions similarly affect the brain's functions, so it is for ease that I use this term as an exemplification.

This book aims to help you deal with your stressed team. To show you how you can influence them to perform well, love their work and want to stay. And if you and your team missed out on the trauma-inducing conditions of the COVID-19 pandemic, don't assume you have escaped the need for change. Or escaped the need to discover how to lead a stressed team. The complex nature of our times alone, with all the new technology and general psychological pressures, warrants a different kind of leadership than you have experienced in the past.

To lead and influence your team to stay requires knowledge about how stress affects people at work. Stressed and disengaged nurses underperform, create interpersonal havoc, and leave. When outer circumstances exert more pressure than you fear you can stand, that's stress. Inner resources don't feel enough to cope with what's happening. It can be acute, experienced as a physical, emotional and mental tension, or as chronic stress lingering over time.

---

3   Dobson et al.

Understaffing is a major cause of chronic stress and results in a downward spiral of disengagement, helplessness and disconnection from quality care and teammates. Your team stop caring, which becomes a safety issue for patient care and their teammates' nursing registrations. The downward spiral leads to more understaffing, with nurses bowing out and quitting because of the pressure. Nurses are leaving in droves because of the impact of chronic stress. And it's not their fault.

Signposts of personal disengagement are not always as easy to see as poor nursing care or sloppy paperwork. Sick leave increases, and disengaged nurses can stop talking with their team. Or they increase talking but it's about finger pointing and disapproval. You may bear the brunt of their criticisms and cliques and drama.

Drama is easy to see. Examples are eye-rolling, avoiding critical conversations, refusing to do tasks, complaining and talking behind people's backs. You might notice they stop talking when you come near. In Darwin in the Northern Territory, Australia, when you're trying to pull somebody else down we call it 'white anting'. Others might say it's passive-aggressive. What this interpersonal havoc does is take people's minds off the job. They're talking about other staff members and complaining about their treatment rather than paying attention to patient care.

It can also be *you* creating drama. You might speak in a manner that distresses a nurse, talk behind a nurse's back, and develop cliques in the team by favouring your friends (often unintentionally). Situations can escalate easily. I have witnessed nurse leaders walk away mid-conversation. They didn't have the skills to deal with a problem. Whatever the personal drama is, it's a distraction from good care. You may find this hard to believe, but if you caused drama unwittingly, it's not all your fault. If you are reading this, you want to do your best. Nurses traditionally don't get taught how to lead and navigate the stumbling blocks along the way. I want to remedy that.

STRESS AND PERFORMANCE

Greta stood in her pantry, her mind was blank, and tears started falling. She couldn't decide what to cook. She'd had a hard day at work and didn't want to make any more decisions. A stressed mind impacts performance, memory and learning. We are hardwired to get stressed, so stress is not always bad. Our bodies go to automatic pilot to help us survive. For example, if we get a scratch, our body knows what to do. We don't say, 'Brain, go and create platelets and the right antibodies to stop infection'. It happens automatically.

Our automatic stress response in fight, flight or freeze mode allows our body to rise to the occasion. Flight is when we need the energy to run or avoid. Fight is if we get aggressive and have to fight to survive. Freeze is when it's too late to run or fight, and your mind goes blank. Unfortunately, these responses that help us survive also affect performance, learning and memory. Think of when you first did a ward round with an imposing consultant. You might have lost your words, been as meek as a lamb, or been defensive. A stressed brain is hypervigilant, looking around for harm, focusing on the negatives or the 'tigers in the bushes'. Your mind is not on the job so it will affect your performance.

The good news is the right amount of stress helps enormously. There is a balance between some pressure and too much. This sweet spot is where you can access the information needed to care for your patients and relate well to others. The Yerkes Dodson performance curve illustrates this relationship between stress and performance. It shows pressure is required to perform, but performance decreases with too much pressure. Greta could not access higher level thinking as her body took over and froze.

The Yerkes-Dodson performance curve

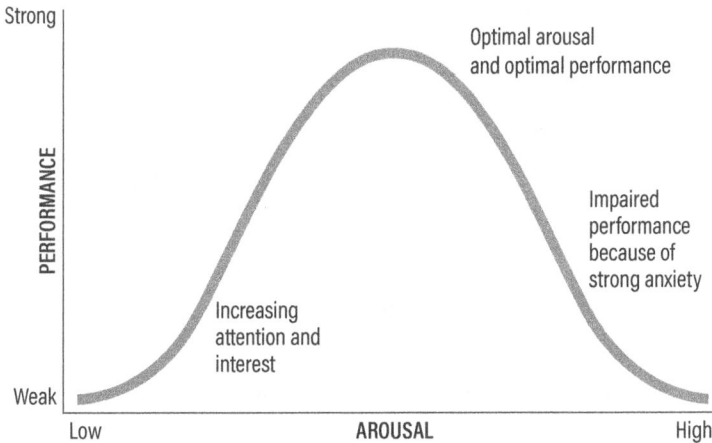

Source: Robert M. Yerkes and John D. Dodson

Even small amounts of stress bypass the prefrontal cortex.[4] An amygdala hijack happens even when a person *thinks* there is a problem! The hijack blocks the complex thinking and decision-making in the front of our brains. Too much stress limits access to the wisdom required to interact well with others.

STRESS AND INTERPERSONAL RELATIONSHIPS

Lyn, a senior nurse, was scared of her charge nurse, Dick. Dick always looked composed, and he kept a poker face. Lyn, who had a warm personality, found this problematic and jumped to

---

4   According to brain studies by Amy Arnsten in 2009.

conclusions about what he thought of her. It stressed her out, and she started to doubt herself.

Stressed minds look for cues to what the problem is. If there is no feedback from their leader, they fill in the gaps with their imagination: *what is this person thinking of me?* Then the nurse at the bedside starts to make assumptions.

As a nurse leader, you control the flow of work and set the unit's tone and culture. You know what happens to children when a mother is having a bad day. It's the same with leaders in charge of the shift. In chapter 2, I will discuss further how your stress level is more important than anybody else's in setting the mood of the day. Nurses at the bedside tell me they lose confidence when their team leader for the day is irritable. They take it personally. Their mind turns to interpersonal drama rather than good patient care.

Ever played sports or watched them? Good leadership can be like having a good umpire. I'd know we had a good netball umpire when I didn't notice them. Their demeanour was clear and crisp, and I could focus on the game as a player. Your performance on the court goes down when you complain about the umpire. Your interpersonal interactions with your team are like this.

Stress makes you reactive. You say and do things you don't mean to, which creates more stress and can affect patient care. When stressed, you are more likely to use command and control mode. Command and control is like the matron of yesteryear – telling people what to do rather than helping them learn, think and problem-solve. It is easy to fall into this trap when feeling time-poor. Your tone may also be abrasive as you have confused assertiveness with aggression. An easy mistake to make early in your career or when you have had role models who have used this type of communication.

Better communication and less drama lead to the nurses in your team being able to focus on the message of your communication and better patient care. If your team starts complaining about how you communicate with them, it takes their mind off the game. And onto you.

Knowing how you affect your team must be paramount for a nurse leader. We explore this in detail in chapter 6. Any stress narrows nurses' focus to the problem, not the solution. It's how the brain is wired. To be unleavable, you need to know what your team wants (chapter 5) to keep them focused on the right things. There's a significant impact on the team when nurses on the floor are disengaged and leave. It's a safety issue. With low nurse numbers on the floor, there's lots of overtime and people take more sick leave, increasing stress. You can spend a lot of time training nurses, and then they leave. It's wise to learn how to keep your nurses in stressful times.

BEING OPEN TO GROWTH

For leaders to be successful they need to be open to learning, growing – and showing up!

I conducted an online leadership training program with four nurse leaders at a small country hospital. One of the leaders was resistant from the start and only attended a quarter of what was offered. At a session on leadership types, she wasn't open to discussing her communication styles or strengths. Everything about her body language was defensive.

The director of nursing said her ward was chaotic and filled with drama, with her team leaving in droves. The other three who attended all the sessions had different experiences and outcomes. They were thrilled with their new insights and skills, and felt more confident about the future.

THE EFFECTS OF POOR MANAGEMENT

When I was researching statistics around retention and engagement, I found claims ranging from 29% to 91% of nurses were considering leaving the profession. Dissatisfaction with management was consistently a key driver for quitting, with poor leadership being the number one motivation to leave. Leadership development must be the primary strategy at an executive and clinical level to rectify the exodus. As a clinical nurse leader, you must learn how to engage and support your team. We are social beings, and relatedness is a part of being human.

It's time to improve your interpersonal skills as a leader to combat 'the other long COVID': the long-term effect on your team from the intensive work period. Ricky Gervais, in the movie *Ghost Town*, played a dentist. He gave a patient sage advice, 'Only floss the teeth you want to keep'. Your new mantra could be, 'Only engage the nurses you want to keep'.

You can start to improve with these four essential skills: self-awareness, self-regulation, social awareness and social regulation. Answer these questions:

Self-awareness: Are you aware when others start to irritate you? What happens in your body?

Self-regulation: Do you give in to the irritation and say how you feel?

Social awareness: Can you notice people's irritation with others or with you?

Social regulation: How can you positively impact the conversation and leave it better than you found it?[5]

---

5   These questions come from 'The Science of Self – Accreditation reference manual for improving emotional intelligence'.

You might think your communication issues are insignificant, like a drop in the ocean of issues. And you may wonder, why bother? Most of the issue is understaffing! Try to think of it like this: every interaction you have with another person is like putting a dollar in their emotional bank account. And focusing on what you can control and influence gives you purpose and a feeling of agency in a world of uncertainty. You take responsibility for your patch.

Researchers Emily Heaphy and Marcial Losada observed 60 management teams as they developed strategic plans. They classified managers' comments as positive or negative, seeking to discover if there was a correlation between these and effectiveness. Effectiveness was measured by financial performance, customer satisfaction and 360-degree feedback of the managers. The ratios of positive to negative comments made the difference between the worst and best performing teams. For medium-performing teams it was 2:1, and for high-performing teams it was 5.6:1. Although other researchers have questioned the maths behind the ratios, this study points towards a tipping point concerning positive and negative comments. Every communication you have with a person makes an impact, and your team will notice if you understand this as you start your transformation to revolutionising your leadership.

Another thought might arise that you shouldn't have to focus on what you say and do. The truth is patient care is affected when nurses focus on interpersonal issues rather than their work. The interpersonal drama also reduces psychological safety as your team won't speak up for fear of reprisal. And in my experience, most leaders don't know when this is occurring!

Is there a situation where interpersonal conflict is beneficial? Yes. Sometimes conflict can be an opportunity to bring up different opinions. New solutions can arise. It also can be an opportunity to grow as a person as it opens you up to hearing how you affect others.

NURSING IN A VUCA WORLD

The US Army War College uses the concept of VUCA to help their senior officers make sense of the challenges they face. VUCA stands for volatile, uncertain, complex and ambiguous. Warren Bennis and Burt Nanus first described VUCA in their book *Leaders: Strategies for taking charge*. Now VUCA is a commonplace term to normalise constant change (volatility); that it's difficult to anticipate what will happen (uncertainty); to describe that problems are multilayered and challenging to understand (complexity); and that there may be no known 'right' answers any more (ambiguity). Living in a VUCA world requires nurse leaders to communicate better to stop turnover.

Nursing in a VUCA world with healthcare crises and challenges also requires agility in learning. Functions of wards and units require repurposing to deal with challenges, and nurses need to leave their specialist areas to care for different types of patients and do new tasks. This calls for a new way to learn and give feedback that doesn't lead to avoidance, stress and damage to the relationship between the leader and clinical nurse (see chapter 7).

Communication

According to editors Jacobus Kok and Barney Jordaan, good communication skills are the number one leadership requirement in this VUCA world. They compiled the work of specialists from different disciplines around the globe into a book named *Leading in a VUCA World*. We, as nurses, are being called to improve our skills and elevate our thinking. Theodore Zeldin, author of *Conversation*, asks, 'When will we have the same breakthroughs in the way we treat each other as we have made in technology?' I like to imagine the time is now, and I am grateful to be your guide.

Communication issues are the leading cause of delays in treatment, higher infection rates and medication errors.[6] Relationship management and clear communication keep your team engaged and performing.

Influence is a critical communication skill, and arguably, influencing others to behave in a particular way is the aim of leadership. Ways to influence are woven through this book, and you will meet the key influential part of you in chapters 6 and 7. Other communication skills are listening skills (chapter 5), understanding how you come across to others (chapters 3 and 5), understanding the emotions behind your communication (chapter 7), picking up on other people's feelings (chapter 4), and listening to what's underneath the words (chapter 4).

Resilience

Resilience is a team sport.

We need each other now more than ever. Leading in a VUCA world is like surfing the big waves with empathy for your fellow surfers. Having a culture of 'we' rather than 'me' is protective. Resilience reduces the risk of moral injury and burnout.[7] Feelings of aloneness come with stress, so increasing relatedness in the ward increases the selfless acceptance of the risk that comes with working in these times.

---

6   According to the Joint Commission on Accreditation of Healthcare Organizations.
7   According to a literature review at the start of 2020 by Bell and Wade.

During the COVID-19 pandemic, the needs of hospitals and the community changed. Nurse leaders needed to think on their feet and change the ward function, but it was difficult for many nurses to see the big picture. Knowing *why* connects actions to a reason and reduces nurses' stress. It falls to leaders to share the reasons why successfully.

Nurses' feeling understood is an important part of their resilience. When I speak to directors or nurse managers, resilience programs are thought to be the answer. But when it comes to training day, the nurses feel resentment as the training feels like a lack of acknowledgement of what they're going through and is implying they are the problem. They say they don't feel seen or heard.

Even when the leadership team does listen, most nurse leaders don't know what to do with what they hear. Jasmine, an outreach child health nurse, regularly visits the communities in Arnhem Land. Listening to the remote nurses' stories and concerns, she feels 'heavier'. She doesn't know what to do for them. You will understand how to handle such situations by the end of this book.

You may consider that you are already empathetic and inclusive and you and your team felt supported through the pandemic. If so, great, but some nurses didn't fare so well. COVID-19 is the first of many shocks as the world is changing quickly. Climate change, threats of war, impacts of global sanctions on the economics of our country and changing finances affect everybody.

The global drama has us all on edge. It's like your engine is always revving too high. You can imagine the impact when your team comes to work and they're on edge. Thinking more about communicating compassionately will help them. In chapter 4, you will discover how to extend compassion to your team and yourself with an easy-to-use formula.

At the start of the pandemic, there was a sense of 'we'. Everybody pitched in and communication was clear. Then, in some cases, this communication dropped off. Then hospital-wide stress levels rose. I heard of nurse leaders saying, 'They should be able to deal with it by now.' This created a toxic culture that infiltrated the conversations and decisions around the team.

Let's use the global COVID-19 pandemic as an example of our VUCA world and consider sharpening our leadership and communication tools using the four key skill areas. Reflect on:

Self-awareness: What was your initial stress response to the changes and disruption at the start of the pandemic? How did it affect your ability to relate to others and perform?

Self-regulation: What did you do to manage your stress? If you had your time again, what would you do differently?

Social awareness: What were other people experiencing? Why do you think they might have been experiencing this? How did it affect their ability to perform?

Social regulation: What did you do to help your team with what they were experiencing? What would you say your consistency was with empathy?

It takes effort to think about questions like these. Self-reflection is a muscle you can build. A simple thing you can do as a leader is to increase your self-awareness, be open to continuous learning, and start to think you could be a leader that's too good to leave.

Purpose as true north

Nurses want to be connected to purpose and come to work for intrinsic reasons. Richard Florida, author of *The Rise of the Creative Class*, said, 'People don't need to be managed. They need to be unleashed.' Purpose is what is meaningful or fulfilling for you. It's the reason why. It's a driving force that gives people the energy to act. Energy is a currency worth chasing and leads to better engagement.

Engagement is often said to be a sense of commitment and job satisfaction. Engaged people appear animated from within, use their strengths, and are more enthusiastic or motivated to go above and beyond because they feel supported.

Millennials and Gen Z are called 'the purpose generation', meaning they need a purpose to become fully engaged in their work.[8] When we use the changes since the pandemic as an example, the 'great resignation' resulted when people questioned their life after the global trauma. Arianna Huffington, listed by Forbes as one of the most powerful women in the world and co-founder of *The Huffington Post* media group and Thrive Global, renamed the great resignation as the 'great re-evaluation'. Humans worldwide want to ensure they're doing what is important to them. Understanding their why helps people decide where to work. Feeling satisfied is a driving force.

Conversations and actions stand out when your brain connects them to your larger purpose. To assist your nursing team to make this connection, ensure you have shared goals you talk about and they can connect with. Show them how they help meet those goals as a group. At the moment, nurses are leaving when work doesn't align with their purpose. Think about when you go to a funeral. You start to evaluate your life: *Am I doing something important to me? Is the stress I'm experiencing at work too much? Should I leave?*

---

8   Millennials were born between 1981 and 1996, while Gen Z was born between 1997 and 2012.

You might think nursing has changed, and we must return to the 'good old days'. It's true. Nursing has changed. The world has changed, and so have you. You've learned, and you've grown and become more confident while you've adapted to many changes. It's easy to look back to the good old days with rose-coloured glasses; in my experience, it's an illusion. The good old days also had issues.

Many people wonder, *I'm not sure if this is my purpose*, like it's a big thing to attain. Thinking it is 'out there' in your future is an error. Your purpose is to feel aligned with values and do what feels right *now*. Looking for one big thing wastes time, rather than accepting what's right in front of you. You can help nurses ground themselves in the small things important to them by linking them each shift with what went well and celebrating small wins.

How do you show your team you value and trust them? Talk to your team about what's important to them. Do you know why they love their job? Do you know what type of patients your team like working with the most? Ask them: what is your reason for working and being in a leadership position (besides money)? Why are those things important to you? Does being good at something affect your motivation? What do you need from your manager to perform well? This last question is important so you understand what your team needs. Knowing this will change the way you act as a leader and make you a leader too good to leave.

Connecting them to their why helps them think about their strengths. It also strengthens your relationship with each nurse. Being connected with your team is a massive part of leadership. It is a buffer for any future interpersonal issues that pop up. It's making deposits in their emotional bank account.

EFFECTIVE NURSING LEADERSHIP STYLES

Our system needs wise leaders who can transform healthcare and influence their teams towards a compelling vision. How do we develop these leaders, and what leadership styles should we use? I have chosen Transformational Leadership and Situational Leadership, for reasons we will discuss throughout this book.

Transformational Leadership is said to be one of the best leadership models for dealing with change: 'Transformational leadership occurs when two or more persons engage with others in such a way the leader and followers raise one another to high levels of motivation and morality.'[9]

Transformational Leadership has also been shown – in a study of 278 nurses and 37 nurse managers – to produce strong leadership effectiveness and outcomes. In the same study, a more transactional leadership style – just giving people tasks – was weakly correlated to leadership satisfaction and effectiveness and did not predict good leadership outcomes. This study, by Jesus Casida and Jessica Parker, found that leaders had to put extra effort into the Transformational Leadership style, but their satisfaction level was higher than when simply being transactional. With healthcare and the world in turmoil, nurses need to use a leadership style that allows their team autonomy – Transformational Leadership does this. Giving nurses choices reduces the impact of a lack of certainty in other parts of their lives and increases their feelings of safety and engagement. (In the next chapter, I will discuss further research to support my reason for choosing this style.)

---

9   Marion Broome and Elaine Sorensen Marshall, *Transformational Leadership in Nursing: From expert clinician to influential leader.*

There are four building blocks of Transformational Leadership:[10]

- **Idealised influence.** Creating respect and trust by being a role model of clinical practice and professionalism, and seeking high standards.
- **Inspirational motivation.** Building a vision and communicating it so the team can see and follow it easily.
- **Intellectual stimulation.** Interacting with the team and being open to others' ideas, new evidence and learning.
- **Individual consideration.** Focusing on being a mentor and coaching leader, and being aware of the team's needs and goals.

Mindset comes before behaviour

You will note that coaching is part of the building blocks of Transformational Leadership. Leadership styles are a good framework to start from but can be challenging to implement. Leadership books and training focus on changing behaviours, but you must also explore the views and beliefs that influence your actions to get results. Otherwise, the new behaviours don't stick. Think about the last time you tried to change a habit. It isn't so easy to stop or start something new.

This idea is shared by the creators of the Health Industry Leadership Capability Assessment (HILCA) and Care Industry Leadership Capability Assessment (CILCA) 360-degree feedback tools. They recognise that mindset comes before behaviour, and awareness is the first step, with transformation as the goal.

---

10   Ibid.

STEP 1	STEP 2	STEP 3
Mindset (view)	Action	Result

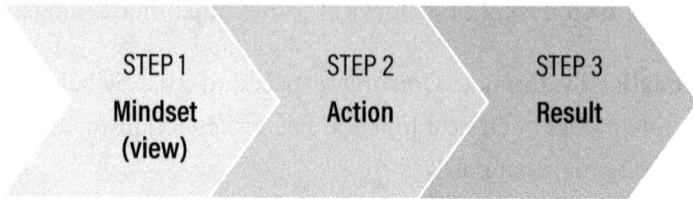

Focusing on the view or mindset of the leader increases the likelihood of long-term and meaningful results. This book focuses on increasing your awareness and exploring what influences your behaviour. In chapter 7, I will share a way to do this that feels easy and authentic and will make you an unleavable leader. And in chapter 9, I share my model – Reflect Forward – that introduces revolutionary new research into behaviour change.

A situational relationship-based model

When I facilitate nurse leadership workshops I run participants through several leadership styles. The leadership style they usually most identify with is Situational Leadership. They explain they tend to adjust their style to the needs of the person and situation. That experience has led me to develop models which combine the research of Transformational Leadership and Situational Leadership, the most common on the floor.

Management consultants and authors Dr Paul Hersey and Ken Blanchard developed in 1969 the original Situational Leadership model. It distinguishes two leadership behaviours: relationship behaviour (supportive) and task behaviour (directional). Dr Hersey refers to the model as 'organised common sense'. Nurses want to lead in a situational way.

The framework I provide takes nursing leadership beyond Transformational Leadership to transformational *relationships*. Transformational relationships are how the magic happens in the unit. It is not about having everyone as a friend or being the most popular. This type of relationship allows nurses to engage with their heads and hearts with you, their team and their work. No one will want to resign, as everybody will feel energised and fulfilled – as much as possible of course, in the challenging healthcare frontline. Leadership is interactive and how you need to lead depends on a number of factors. I've taken it a step further in the new model, Transformational Nurse Identities. It depends on your mindset and actions and how it interacts with another's mindset and actions.

The mapping of Transformational Leadership I introduce in chapter 7 is effective, practical and grounded in sound theories, and I have taught this to many nurse leaders. The rest of this book explores how to implement the inner leadership and interpersonal aspects when the rubber hits the road, every shift. Nursing leadership development needs to be practical, not theoretical and not just task-focused. It also needs to be an interactive model.

Activating transformational relationships

There need to be followers for you to be a leader. You can't be a leader unless somebody buys into the idea, states Simon Weston, author of *Leadership*. Activating your team to do the work is a leader's goal. Awareness of your communication and behaviour styles is a way to be in the 'right relationship' with your followers.

Imagine a two-paned window. The left side is clear as it symbolises how you and your team can see your behaviour and communication style. The pane to the right is blacked out only to you. Others can see what you can't. This model of what is seen and unseen by an individual is called a Johari Window, created by Joseph Luft and Harrington Ingham. It's a way to understand that others see more of you than you think. You can discover some parts of this blacked out pane by getting feedback. Self-awareness tools such as leadership inventories are other ways.

Tasha Eurich, a researcher on self-awareness, discovered 95% of us think we are self-aware, but in actuality only 10% to 15% of us are. Her studies show these 10% to 15% have higher levels of fulfilment, perform better at work, and have stronger relationships as they are better at communicating. They are also more confident. It's also empowering and allows you to improve your leadership as you become more agile to be who you need to be to keep yourself and your team engaged.

It can be scary to uncover what others see. Try to start gently: ask three people close to you what they think your strengths are. What do they think your challenges are?

Ask clarifying questions if required. Then thank them without comment or getting defensive.

CONCLUSION

Our times require an unprecedented type of leadership. You have now learned not to underestimate the impact of stress. You know it gets in the way of how well you and others work individually and as a team. You have also become more aware of how your behaviour could affect others, and that a missing piece of the leadership puzzle could be forming transformational relationships. You have started your journey into exploring how Transformational Leadership and Situational Leadership styles are what nurses want, and that they predict good nursing outcomes. You've also increased your level of awareness. Well done.

You can let go of any blame around the chaos that is healthcare. Everyone is doing their best in extreme circumstances. Be open to the idea that you can use relational skills to transform yourself and your team and it will be easier than you think.

In the next chapter, we start where you are – a knowledgeable clinical leader trying your best to implement new leadership styles – and discuss how this can sometimes get in the way of engaging your team. You will learn about emotional intelligence to frame a way to look at communicating effectively. When you understand that we are a tribe at heart, you will see what is expected in this new way of leading. You'll also discover the common obstacles to being the best leader you can be, setting up a self-development plan we carry forward in this book.

2

Getting to know yourself and others

UNDERSTANDING EMOTIONAL INTELLIGENCE

You may already think you have good awareness. Most of us believe we are conscious, logical beings. But in this chapter, I'll show that your responses are automatic 98% of the time. They're coming from past emotions and experiences rather than how you need to act in the present. If nurse leaders do not get a handle on this, they respond to their teams and make decisions that are not relevant or helpful. One way to get this new awareness and skills comes from improving your emotional intelligence (EI). Knowledge of the aspects of EI that create transformational relationships will uplevel your leadership.

You have been practising EI skills already! In the previous chapter, I introduced the four aspects of emotional intelligence: self-awareness, self-regulation, social awareness and social regulation. Daniel Goleman, psychologist and international business consultant, first popularised emotional intelligence with his book *Emotional Intelligence: Why it can matter more than IQ*. He later described its utility further in his book *The New Leaders: Transforming the art of leadership into the science of results*. Emotional intelligence is the capacity to be aware of your own and others' emotions, and being able to regulate them to meet your goals and influence people. Emotions drive behaviours and so are necessary to understand.

Many compelling studies connect EI with Transformational Leadership (TL) in nurses. One study demonstrated that EI was significantly positively correlated with TL.[1] Furthermore, extra effort, effectiveness and satisfaction were significantly negatively correlated with laissez-faire leadership. Bernard Bass (2006) describes laissez-faire leadership as an absence of leadership with a hands-off approach. Many nurse tasks are routine, and you can leave your nurses to get on with it. This isn't laissez-faire. This is trust. No matter the level of trust, rounding on patients is said to be becoming best practice in US hospitals, says Rose O Sherman, nurse leadership author of *The Nurse Leader Coach*. It doesn't mean you don't trust your team – it shows care and interest. Rose goes on to say that it is beneficial for patients and staff, and it allows the nurse leaders to have coaching conversations and improves patient safety.

You might wonder if you engage in transformational relationships already, or perhaps you are rushing around too much. You are not alone. Compassion is a nursing hallmark, but task allocation often wins over making connections. Heavier workloads, the complexity of tasks and increased managerial pressure impact leadership.[2]

---

1   By Lauraine Spano-Sxekely, Mary T Quinn Griffin, Joanne Clavelle and Joyce J Fitzpatrick.
2   Mary Dixon-Woods et al. (2014) in 'Culture and Behaviour in the English National Health Service' state that leaders may focus on tasks over strategies to motivate staff and improve performance.

The missing critical skill

I've done dozens of nurse emotional intelligence inventories, and the critical skill that's often missing is social regulation. Nurses are great at noticing the feelings of others. Some nurse leaders I've spoken to say they are attuned more to their patients' emotions and needs than their team's. Is it the same for you?

On an emotional intelligence inventory, a team leader in a medical ward scored high on activities with social awareness skills, but her score for social regulation was much lower than average. This low score meant she didn't know how to use the information she had received as cues from others. If she saw uncertainty or distress on someone's face she didn't know what to do next. The confusion led to a lack of confidence and second-guessing herself. She was also second-guessing her clinical knowledge.

But a low social regulation score doesn't always come from not knowing what to do. Another senior in the same ward had low social awareness and social regulation. When we unpacked that, she was angry at the executive team and felt they didn't care. She'd stopped trying, and had shut down. Could this be burnout? Maybe. Whatever the reason, she was causing havoc. She had the ear of many staff, and her complaining created unrest and stoked the fires of an already negative and dissatisfied culture. She was short with the team and barked orders at people, and many didn't want to work with her.

THE KNOWLEDGE TRAP

It may surprise you, but just focusing on clinical knowledge can blind you. When nurse leaders do not understand they have to activate their team to get the best out of them, they can end up alienating others. It's easy when busy to take shortcuts and give orders. Giving orders is Transactional Leadership. Daniel Goleman, the psychologist and consultant who made EI accepted, calls this 'autocratic leadership' in his book *The New Leaders*. Giving your team orders does not enable them to become critical thinkers or inspire them to work at a higher level.

This is the managing style I talked about in the previous chapter – command and control – where you just want to get the job done. In the old days, this was called being a manager. There is nothing wrong with managing; many of a nurse leaders' tasks are management tasks. Leadership in medicine and nursing was taught and practised like the military style of command and control. Telling people what to do is an effective way to manage people in a crisis; as already noted, it is still a relevant style at times.

But we are discussing in this book broadening your skillset to become the type of leader rarely seen or aspired to. Creating transformational leadership and relationships is the goal. It's a 'doing with' rather than a 'doing to' leadership, creating a synergistic response where the sum of two parts equals a much greater output. To accomplish this, the power differential in the unit needs to shift, and you and your team must become healthcare partners.

It's not your knowledge that makes them stay

Think about those shifts where you felt valued by seniors. I can remember mine. One of them was in the late 1990s on night duty in the ICU at the Royal Darwin Hospital. A patient was haemorrhaging so much that blood was running off the bed onto the floor. The nurse in charge and the registrar were at the bedside with me all night. I was pumping blood into the patient and we were bouncing ideas off each other. Though the patient was critical, it was one of my favourite shifts. We were in flow. Flow means there was pressure on us, and we were stretched, but we felt we could handle it. The salient part was how we worked together. I felt like a valued part of the team, and I went over and above.

Contrast that with another shift in ICU with my friend Deb, who was allocated a sick baby. The nurse in charge came to the bedside to check some drugs and ventilator settings. Later in the evening, the charge nurse was dismissive of Deb when she wanted to escalate some concerns around ventilation. The nurse in charge continued laughing with her friends at the nurses' station, and Deb lost a learning experience. This example of poor leadership left Deb feeling stressed, unseen and unrespected.

A minor, insignificant incident to a nurse leader can feel enormous to a nurse at the bedside. Was the nurse in charge knowledgeable and right about saying Deb need not be worried? Yes.

Now you can see both sides in this example, what do you see as the issue here? What could the nurse leader have done better?

The Transformational Leadership of the registrar and nurse leader in my example from over 25 years ago is still significant in my mind. Their treatment of me was that special, something that enabled me to perform well. This sort of leadership behaviour improves the culture of the ward, leads to better patient care and provides memories like the one I have described. Respecting others will keep people engaged and wanting to come to work.

They also have a degree

Your team does need to keep standards, but we also want them to be more than robots taking orders. You have a thinking team who must learn critical thinking skills. Take Mary. She is one of the nurses I've been coaching recently. Her manager had asked her to go onto permanent night duty and be a team leader but Mary didn't want to. She lacked confidence. When we dug deeper, we found a culture of autocratic leadership at her work – *do what I say* – which doesn't lead to excellent succession planning. Mary wasn't the only one who didn't want to step up.

Meet Ashlee, an educator in a major city operating theatre. Ashlee is a nurse who always wants to improve and puts what she learns into practice. Our topic for one session was giving feedback and how to empower the team to find their own answers. The day after, Ashlee emailed me with excitement:

> *I just have to share, have just had the most profound conversation using feedforward with a junior nurse! I was able to open up the conversation by asking how she felt about the case, following up with anything she could improve on, which was being more prepared, so I delved in and asked if she had any ideas on how to be more prepared, with no answer. I asked if I could give her some ideas to be more prepared and then when she said yes, I told her. Then the conversation ended with a big thank you from her.*
>
> *FELT AMAZING! Feeling a tonne more confident in using this in real-life situations, so a big thank you to you!*

She had treated the junior nurse like a thinking person and didn't just tell her what to do. I devote a whole chapter to this – you will get some scripts for feedforward and transformational coaching conversations in chapter 8.

As a leader, you are often the primary knowledge holder on the shift. Sometimes you *do* need to tell people what to do in a critical situation or when you're time-poor. But it's also about *how* you tell them. You know this, I know this, we all know this. But the application of it … well, we know sometimes we slip a bit.

I have a few hints on how to consistently do this well. It's about your perspective on your team and your level of stress in that moment. It is also about how you think of yourself concerning the other person at that moment. Are you respecting the other person? What is your assumption? Are you blaming them? Are you annoyed at someone else when you are talking to them? Do you think they are stupid (hard to admit, even to yourself!)? More on this later in the chapter (and virtually every chapter, as it's so important).

Are you trying to empower your team and get them to come up with the answers, as Ashlee did in the transformational coaching model? Start to notice what you do already to help others learn and do their job well. For example, do you ask questions? Do you ask them what they need? Or what is working well for them today or with that patient?

Start to take note of even your body language. Are you smiling, or is your tone conversational? Are you coming to every conversation with respect? Do you think you have a bias against some people and talk to them differently? Do you look at the person and use their name? Do you come back and check on them – closing the loop in a conversation? These are all excellent ways to communicate, and they count.

THE ELEMENTS OF EMOTIONAL INTELLIGENCE

Emotions are behind our actions, no matter how rational we feel. The origin of the word emotion is French, 'emouvior', meaning 'a social moving, stirring, agitation'. The Latin root for motivation, movement and emotion is 'emovere'. Inspiring others is a key transformational nursing skill requiring you to tap into feelings.

When Simon Weston discusses leadership, he insists there needs to be a bridge between theories of leadership and making things practical. Emotional intelligence is one way to do this. EI is also a predictor of Transformational Leadership in nurse managers.

In a healthcare environment, Mary Johanson, author of the article 'Keeping the Peace: Conflict management strategies for nurse managers', says our relationships are complicated, and emotions are present in patients, families and staff. Leaders need skills to deal with everyone's feelings, including their own. When you are stressed you shift into the 'doing to' transactional leadership style rather than the 'doing with' transformational leadership style.

Start to practise self-awareness of your leadership behaviours now:

- Do you have to reduce your stress response before you talk to people?
- Do you notice their response when you talk to some of your team members?
- Do you adapt and change depending on what you are noticing?

Start with being objective and notice what you do. It may feel clunky. Permit yourself to try anyway. Pausing and reflecting can feel like it takes up a lot of energy to start with, but it will get much easier over time. Then you'll begin to notice what you're doing while doing it.

It sounds great when you read the theory of Transformational Leadership, but how do you make it practical? A very experienced nurse manager aimed to get her team to improve performance in the unit by giving more timely and better feedback. She knew what to do, and she tried to teach them. It didn't work. They would still avoid giving feedback. It's the same if you're a team leader with a complaint. It can be difficult to change if you don't understand the elements lacking in the first place. Sometimes knowledge of what to do isn't enough. A missing piece is who you need to BE to do the actions. Part of that is emotional intelligence.

How to improve your social regulation

Not being taught the correct elements of EI means you can't always effectively apply your leadership knowledge. It's not your fault, as EI isn't often taught to nurses, although in speaking to other health-care leadership consultants, nurses finally want more support to do this challenging role. Nurses can be masterful communicators with patients. They're warm, open and friendly, but we know there are four components to EI. From my research and experience, the missing element is often social regulation.

Social regulation is knowing what you could or should do in a situation to help someone else. Getting someone to take action is much easier when you use appropriate communication. Some people are better at communication and building up aspects of EI. However, even those people get a lot better with skill building. Building EI muscles takes time, self-reflection and practice.

Let's start with developing some social awareness:

- Be curious about others and get to know your team when you don't have time constraints. Ask them about what they're doing on the weekend, or if they have a dog. Ask them more about it and show them you care. Make it a lightly personal question.

- Watch someone whose relationship skills you admire and list what they do.

The best question to ask yourself to improve your social regulation is, 'How can I positively impact this situation to leave it better than I found it?' After reading this book, you will have some knowledge about this, but it's still a helpful question now.

And try asking this of yourself before every interaction: 'How can I empower my team?'

You can also ask others questions to increase your self-awareness. Ask those you admire to give you feedback on your body language and communication style. You need to know these hidden parts of you to increase the corresponding square in the Johari Window and increase your self-awareness.

The last tip for now is to be accountable and find ways to make up after a negative interaction. Bell, an experienced nurse on the late shift, escalated a perceived safety issue via email about Joanne's early shift. Bell emailed her Nurse Unit Manager, Mark, and included the quality nurse and another associate nurse manager. She had not included Joanne, the nurse in charge of the early shift, or talked to her about the issue. What Bell had said was valid, but the process she went through hurt Joanne and left her angry and embarrassed in front of the other senior nurses. Joanne resented Bell and lost some confidence.

In this example, what do you think Bell could have done instead? What about Mark? How could he have handled it? Or Joanne?

Another case study: a community-controlled health centre had an issue. The team had lost trust in their clinical leaders. The leaders listened well to complaints or recommendations around clinical care but didn't close the loop. They missed an essential step the team needed to feel their ideas are important. Get back to your team with an outcome, even if it isn't the desired one. It doesn't matter if you can't always act on your team's initiatives. It does matter if you don't tell them the outcome. They will trust you more when you close this communication loop.

Nobody wants a complaint from misreading a situation. When they get a complaint, many nurse team leaders start to second guess themselves and lose confidence. Receiving a complaint and not having the right skills for how to handle the complaint increases your stress. It's worth getting communication situations right the first time.

You may already have excellent communication skills. Even if you do, if you keep reading and learn something that prevents a nurse complaint and helps your relationship with your team, it's worth it.

THE SURPRISING IMPACT OF CONSCIOUS AND UNCONSCIOUS THINKING

A key aspect of emotional intelligence is emotional literacy. Being able to name your emotions leads to self-awareness and assists with emotional regulation. An extension of this is being able to map your emotions and behaviours over time and in response to others – naming aspects of yourself and seeing how they change depending on who you are with, the situation and what sort of mood or mindset you are in. One way to understand yourself and your reactions to your environment is to see yourself as a multifaceted personality, consisting of parts. You may already say to yourself or hear others say that a 'part of them' wanted to do something, but another part wanted to do something entirely different. Understanding parts of yourself is essential to understanding the interaction effect of leading others, and to ensure your ideal self is able to lead your team rather than the reactive self that leads from stressed, unconscious parts. Let's explore this flexible and practical way of seeing yourself and others that will show you how you can transform your relationships and revolutionise your leadership.

The different parts of you

Your leadership journey started when you were a child. It's hard to believe. You learned how to be a leader by watching other leaders. The leaders were your coaches, parents, teachers and even first managers. They all trained you how to be a leader. Most of the time, when you're led, you don't know why you're doing the things you're doing. Discovering your influences gets interesting because you've got multiple leadership examples interacting with your personality style. Inside you, you've got these different parts to help you lead.

You also have some parts that are triggered from experiences with others. These can cause interpersonal issues with your team and stress you. Nurse leaders are often confused about why they try to lead with the best intentions but people 'push their buttons'. Our brains operate like high-fidelity recorders for our experiences, even before birth.[3] People or situations can trigger these stored experiences. Eric Berne, a renowned psychotherapist, calls these interactions between us and others 'transactions' and named his model Transactional Analysis. The bits that react with another are called 'parts', 'states' or 'selves'. This way of thinking about our relationships with others became very popular in the 1970s. The book that extends Berne's model of Transactional Analysis,

---

3   According to the pioneering work of brain surgeon Wilder Penfield.

I'm OK – You're OK by Thomas Harris, was on the *New York Times* bestseller list in 1972. Harris explained the findings as follows:

> *Persons can exist in two states at the same time. The patient knew he was on the operating table talking with Penfield; he was seeing the 'Seven-up Bottling Company … and Harrison Bakery'. He was dual in that he was at the same time in the experience and outside of it, observing it.*

When different parts of the brain were stimulated, discrete memories arose. That's why people – nurses in your team – can remind you of somebody else, and they can annoy you, even though you don't know why. Their behaviour annoys you because they sometimes remind you of somebody else. Or they trigger your stress response and you get defensive. You are existing in this moment with your teammate – annoyed – but you equally are back in time with an automatic response from a memory of a transaction of annoyance. We cover these transactions in more detail in chapter 5 and, in the words of a client, 'once seen, it can't be unseen'.

The different systems of thinking

Nobel Laureate Daniel Kahneman, known for behavioural economics, outlines two systems of thinking in his book *Thinking, Fast and Slow*. System one is unconscious thinking, and 98% of the time we come from this automatic way of thinking. We like this way of thinking as it's fast and effortless. System one thinking is the part of you that loves command and control. You know what to do, and you tell someone else the answer to the problem.

System two thinking is different. It's slower. You have to use some effort and the logical front part of your brain. It's there for more complicated problems; you can see patterns from this part of your mind. This system is deliberate about your actions and interpersonal relationships.

Linking the parts and systems

System one thinking uses information from the past, and system two thinking is deliberately using thinking for novel situations. A complex VUCA world requires system two thinking. System two thinking allows you to be objective and see where you can improve, and will help revolutionise your leadership. You might think, *I've got no time for slow thinking, just fast.* System one thinking helps you make quick clinical decisions on things you know well, but there needs to be a balance between fast and slow. Reflection is a significant skill to cultivate and requires system two thinking. We do not learn from experience, we learn from reflecting on experience.[4] We will talk more about intentionally using reflective practice in chapter 9. To get new behaviours to be automatic, you must first go slow and repeat them. Go slow now to go fast later.

Uncovering your biases

There's an unconscious bias test from Harvard Education to explore your system one thinking.[5] I did it, and I was surprised to discover that I had a slight bias on the subject of gender and career. This is valuable information for me – you'd think it's a no-brainer that women should be as entitled as men to a career, especially as I am a woman with a career!

---

4   According to learning expert John Dewey.
5   https://implicit.harvard.edu/implicit/.

Locating yourself

Every leader needs to discover where they formed their leadership approaches. Think back to your coaches', your teachers' and even your parents' style of communicating and using power.

How did they communicate with other people? How did they use power? How did they handle their emotions or those of others? How did they get people to do things? How did your first nursing leaders, clinical nurse managers or nurse unit managers treat you when you were younger? How have they influenced you? Was there a critical incident in your early nursing career or leadership journey where you decided to lead in a particular way? Find some words for this to locate what you think a leader is and how you feel a leader should act and be.

Answer this question:

Social awareness: Have you ever noticed people shift and change before your eyes? One minute they are calm, and the next teary or energised or annoyed. You may see it in yourself. In chapter 5, I will present a system of selves that will be the game changer for your self-awareness.

AT HEART, WE ARE A TRIBE

A leader's reactivity impacts the team more than anybody else's stress response. In psychology, we call reactivity a level of arousal or stress – how you go from 0 to 10.

You may have noticed that if someone experiences stress around you, you are more likely to feel it too. You pick it up with your mirror neurons, turning on your stress response. (When scientists mapped brain cell functions in monkeys, mirror neurons were found by accident. The same neurons fired when the monkey grasped a banana as when they watched the experimenter grab it.) Your team will sense another's stress using their mirror neurons, and it affects them in a negative way. Understanding this gives you motivation as a team leader to be more composed at work and act with your team in mind.

Imagine there's a tribe of gorillas lazing in the jungle, and you are the head gorilla. You are on the lookout to keep your tribe safe. You think you see a threat in the distance and become anxious. The tone of the tribe changes and becomes vigilant, as they know it's the head gorilla's job to keep them safe. Any bystander would see signs of stress, agitation and gossip among the tribe. This scenario also happens at your workplace. You are the head gorilla. If you are stressed, the impact is more significant than if anyone else is.

This phenomenon also works in your favour. As the head of the tribe, when you are less stressed, you'll impact your team in a good way. When the COVID-19 pandemic was at its height, I know managers were trying to be calm because they said, 'We've got this in hand. We can do this.' It then gave the belief to everybody else. It's a high-leverage activity for a leader to learn how to be composed in the face of stress. The team looks at you and thinks, 'Oh, my leader must know something I don't know, and I'm going to trust that.' It also works for engagement. An engaged leader creates an engaged team. You can't support the intrinsic motivation in another if it doesn't exist in you. If you are complaining that your team isn't motivated, check your level of engagement to see if you are part of the problem.

You might worry about being responsible for your team's feelings and responses. You are not responsible for anybody else's feelings but your own. But you do need to learn the impact of your feelings. We've all been on a ward where excuses are made for bad behaviour. Someone says, 'Oh, that's just them.' But we all know it's not good enough. Brain scans show when somebody witnesses an act of unfairness to another person, it lights up the part of the brain that experiences pain. We are social creatures wired to help and look after each other.

Sometimes it's good to show your team your stress response and be honest. It allows you to be relatable, and your team will feel more connected to you. But it would be best if you were intentional about doing this. Pay more attention to your stress response by using self-awareness, and then you can regulate it. For example, you can do box breathing in a moment of stress. You can also make sure you rest well and are a good model for self-care. Talk about what you do for self-care and not about self-destructive behaviours like excessive drinking.

You can try box breathing, which is used by SAS forces and pilots to reduce their stress response in critical moments. Breath in for four seconds, hold for four, breath out for four, hold for four, and repeat three more times.

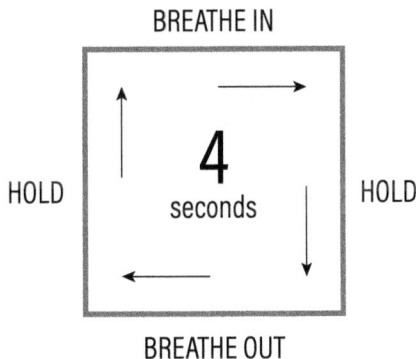

BREATHE IN

HOLD

4
seconds

HOLD

BREATHE OUT

Box breathing helps by shifting the focus from the stress to counting, which is one mechanism to turn the stress response off. Another method is slowing the breath and holding it. These techniques are very powerful, and I've used them successfully when I've had to speak in front of hundreds of people at conferences to calm my nerves.

Some nurses are great at boundary setting with their time, and some have blank looks when we talk about self-care. They don't know how. More than one nurse I know of has had a hard time putting themselves first. They are parents, nurses and team leaders. They manage everything. They were never taught to be kind to themselves and make their care matter. We all know about putting your mask on first if the plane's going down. You need to start asking yourself, *what do I like to do?* and notice the feelings in your body when you do it. That's self-care. It's also self-care when you show self-compassion. We will cover this in chapter 4.

Another question you might ask is, *does it make a difference to my team if I'm running around flustered?* The short answer is yes. Ask any stressed mother if it rubs off on the kids – we know it does.

> Reflect on:
>
> **Social awareness:** Have you noticed your impact on your team when you communicate? Have you noticed the energy shift in your team as a result of your conversations with them?

CONCLUSION

This chapter has opened you up to the idea that your leadership journey began well before you started leading. These leadership habits you developed are parts inside you with different leadership ideas; some will interact negatively with your team and get in the way of your progress as a leader. Learning about the aspects of EI and developing these skills will remedy this to help your thinking thrive. You have learnt that you have two systems of thinking – fast and slow – and although the quick system is energy efficient, it is not enough to depend on in the complex world of healthcare. Lastly, you have discovered that your stress response matters more than anyone else's, and it's worthwhile to cultivate good self-care and ways to stay composed each day.

Stop thinking you've got too much work to develop yourself as a leader. Humans are complex, and change happens over time. Start to take your wellbeing, leadership development and stress management more seriously. Your ability to deal with people is crucial, and you can do it step by step – one new awareness, one new action at a time.

In the next chapter, we'll ask, 'Shouldn't I just be myself?' and start to map out parts of the unconscious selves, including the parts involved with leadership, to discover how they came about and their functions. You're going to learn that in your role, you need to start to be picky about which parts you use and how being intentional helps your leadership.

3

Shouldn't I just be myself?

WHY BEING AUTHENTIC CAN BE A MISTAKE

'Be yourself as everyone else is already taken.' This quote is often touted as coming from Oscar Wilde. In this age of freedom, individuality and personal development we are encouraged to embrace and celebrate our differences. Leadership theory is no different. Authentic Leadership is also a valid nursing leadership model.

Authentic Leadership and Transformational Leadership are both examples of relational styles. Both are said to improve nursing practice. Relational style is just as it sounds – focusing on relationships to achieve excellence in healthcare. Authenticity gives you a unique voice that shows you are genuine, trustworthy and believable. Being *you* in your leadership allows you to be honest and open in your relationships with other people. Your integrity shines through as you speak with a clear voice. Another benefit of Authentic Leadership is the high self-awareness required to lead this way. When you lead from an original, motivated and engaged place, you're more energetic and aligned with your values and your team is more likely to follow.

What's unspoken is how relying on authenticity can be dangerous. The authentic voice tells you to go with your gut and act from who you think you are – missing the element of context. It relies on a high level of self-awareness and self-regulation that many don't have. Behaving how you feel can be dangerous. For example, when trying to get a task done and someone interrupts, feelings of overwhelm and irritation may arise. You feel it is authentic to share your displeasure with others when they ask you how you're going. You take it out on other people because it feels right. Being authentic can be a mistake as it gives you permission to be reactive and throw your irritability and annoyance around.

In some ways, it's energy efficient to go with what you feel because you don't have to override your emotions and think from a higher level. However, decision-making from a higher level is needed to maintain relationships and keep your mind functioning on all cylinders.

Emotional reasoning is what we call a 'cognitive distortion'. Emotional reasoning happens when you think through the feelings being experienced at the moment. Cognitive distortion describes a distorted form of thinking. If you feel low, you judge the day as going badly or the person you are with as annoying. When emotional reasoning is around, you take your feelings as truth rather than using critical thinking. It's an example of system one thinking, which we discussed in chapter 2. We have said that it helps us make quick decisions but also leads to interpersonal issues.

Reactivity isn't just saying something you regret. Walking away from a discussion before it's finished can also be reactive. Avoiding tough conversations like this can appear inconsistent to others and risk psychological safety. And you lose trust.

Despite doing the same job, nurses' personalities are different. Each personality type has contrasting objectives, work preferences and communication styles. You might be a big picture thinker, warm and engaging, but you might have a detail-oriented team member who doesn't like rapport-building chit-chat. It can be confusing, as there are contrasting leadership and personality styles. There is no wrong or right way to be a leader. How do you know who you need to be at each moment?

In this chapter, you'll begin to understand why you behave as you do. We'll discuss how living a good life and being a great leader means picking the parts of you that lead the best in the moment. And you will start your 'leadership dashboard'. A leadership dashboard is a tool that tracks important elements of your leadership. Use it is an opportunity to gain clarity on your goals, values, strategies, communication plans and so on. Then you can focus on what matters. In this chapter, you'll also discover the five aspects of making a deliberate choice, which help you choose how to act authentically and appropriately – enabling you to make what is generally reflexive more deliberate. This increases your chances of success.

A colleague of mine conducted a leadership inventory with a nursing leader who worked in outpatients. Despite getting objective feedback from this and input from her team about her behaviour, she discounted it all. Instead she listened to her inner promptings to behave as she had always done. This felt right to her as it was her natural inclination. She found it easier to be direct to the point of rudeness rather than take feedback, take a breath and take a softer, gentler approach.

Nurses can be promoted because they have this direct, task-oriented style rather than a people orientation. The DISC inventory, which looks at behaviours and communication styles, defines an 'adaptive' and 'natural' style. The adaptive style is when an individual can shift their everyday work style to adapt to the environment in their role. I've done many of these inventories with nursing executives at a high level. They've had to become more detail-oriented and systems-oriented to thrive at work. They had a natural style that was low detail but adapted their style to suit the role. It is possible, with insight, to change and adjust for the type of work you need to do. But generally, when you're working on the floor and with people, you need to bring your focus to relationships, not just tasks.

You have already shifted your attention to behave differently when it counts. Take your mind back to a cold winter morning, feeling snug and warm in bed. You might discover that you focus on how you feel. This causes you to resist getting up. Notice what happens when you shift your attention to the consequences of staying in bed too long. Feelings of discomfort arise with remembering your commitments. It's only then that you discover it's easy to get moving. You shifted from a sense of comfort to your values and what was important.

You can do the same when you are feeling reactive. When you are annoyed, it draws your attention. With awareness you can shift your attention to what is important: your values. Alternatively you can shift your attention to another's strengths, your goals or who you have decided to be as a leader. Then deciding what to do next is more effortless. To increase self-awareness and self-regulation, try this for yourself.

To revolutionise your leadership you need to evolve as a person and leader. Nothing else will work unless this occurs. Now let's explore how your personality was formed and how it interacts with your team in helpful and unhelpful ways.

THE FORMING OF YOU

So far you have discovered that you already lead with different parts of you. You learnt how from your past experiences. I will now provide a model to further describe how your parts evolve. I invite you to imagine your personality as a circle (shown below). The little circles inside it are parts of you. These parts evolved from childhood, resulting from the combination of your DNA and interactions with your environment. Think of these circles as symbolic. Paul Federn, a psychoanalyst who studied under Freud, named these parts 'ego states'.

The different parts of you

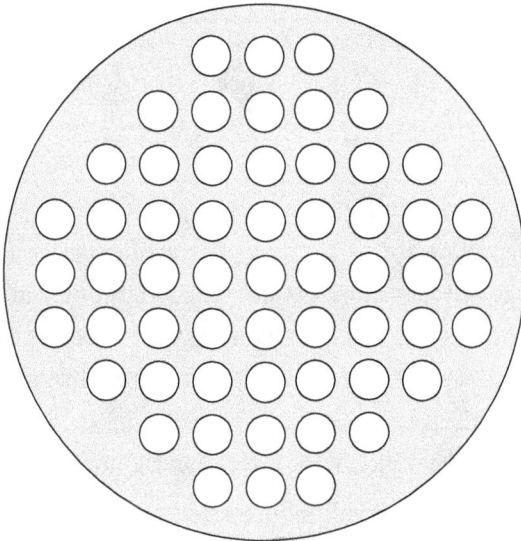

Imagine you are a baby, lying in your cradle. Near you is a loved caregiver. You smile at them, and they smile back. A part of you realises, *if I'm nice to these people, say yes to them, I get more of what I want.* The part of you that we call 'the pleaser' is now developing. There will be many of you with well-developed pleasers reading this book.

But we also contain the opposite facet. What is a two-year-old's favourite word? It's 'no'. The boundary-setting part of you is now developing. Imagine a two-year-old putting on their unicorn magic fairy boots to go to the shops, and mum wants them to wear their runners. 'No, I want to wear my magic fairy boots to the shops.' If mum says okay, then this part of you will develop. If you get to say no and have a say about what is important to you, knowing what you like and what is good for you comes easy and you have no trouble with boundaries and saying no to others. However, in my experience, the opposite is usually the case. If you're in an environment that encourages being a 'people pleaser', you start to be a 'nice' person. You have trouble saying no and find it hard to connect to your own needs and what is important to you. This can become your identity and how you relate to others. But remember, you will have both parts inside you. It's all about context and when you use each part.

To help understand this concept, consider *Inside Out*, an animated Pixar movie. The movie is experienced through an 11-year-old girl, Riley, and the parts of her that help her make decisions. These parts are anger, sadness, joy, fear and disgust. Unlike the movie, the parts we will discuss in you consist of thoughts, feelings, actions and images in your mind. They have discrete memories and values.

Let's think of the development of other parts. Take the introvert and the extrovert. There is probably a part of you that loves going to parties, seeing people, going out for dinner and hanging out outside the house. But another part of you also likes nothing more than sitting at home on the couch, reading a book, watching Netflix or having some quiet time. You need a balance inside you. If this extrovert party person made you go out all the time, it would burn you out regardless of what overall personality type you think you are.

When things aren't going so well, you will have an imbalance between your parts. One of your parts will be 'running the show'. Sometimes parts are created by your personality to make a balanced way of moving through the world. A method of surviving. Parts of your personality are there to help you, and once you understand them it's a matter of choosing the parts of you that lead the best.

Some of these unconscious parts are not always useful, unless you're mindful and know they're there. Think about when you catch up with your siblings or parents and fall into old habits. These are old, unconscious behaviours.

Another way to look at this is to consider these various parts as being effective or not when considering a specific goal. 'Executive state identification' is a process created by Jan Sky. She gives many examples of this process in her book *The Many Parts of You*. First, you make a map of your parts. Then you:

1. Name your goal.
2. Map out parts of you that inhibit your goal.
3. Map out the parts that assist you with your goal.

I love this tool so much that I joined with Jan and formed a company, and we worked together for some years.

Try it yourself. Look at who you need to be to meet your goal. You can name your parts anything, including people's names. In the early days I admired a leader called Sharon. She was a straight talker but very kind and knowledgeable. So I had a part called Shaz. Don't overthink it, as you are just starting. Make your own rules and get creative.

What part do you need to come from to fulfil the purpose of being a transformational leader and engage your team?

If you need to be more assertive – you'd come from the boundary setting part of you that says no. Be assertive but not aggressive.

If you are oppositional all the time, you would consider another part and be open.

If you talk more than you listen you need to come from a quieter, more curious part.

Coming from a part of you gives you the formula to do what's right in the moment because each moment is different and needs a different approach. You can choose the parts of you to lead from and still be authentic. You can still be yourself.

Developing yourself can reduce vulnerability and make you feel more powerful in your work. In the book *Embracing Our Selves*, renowned psychotherapists Hal Stone and Sidra Winkleman describe how our personalities evolve. This process helps you grow as a person and also as a leader. It'll make you feel more confident. Understanding yourself means you have more personal power and agency over your choices. It's then easier each day to think of which parts you need to come from to meet your goals and empower your team. This will help to reduce the overwhelm that comes with leading in healthcare today.

Thinking that you have 'parts' can be confusing. You just feel like you. The mind is a complex system that manages to lump our perceptions together to make us feel like a coherent self. As mentioned earlier, sometimes you feel extroverted and want to go to a party. Other times you want to be alone and read a book. Both are parts of you. I know this is a challenging idea when you're not used to thinking of yourself like that. Some of my clients worry they might have schizophrenia when I first introduce parts to them.

But schizophrenia is a mental disorder characterised by delusions, hallucinations, disorganised thoughts, and disorganised speech and behaviour. These individuals have an altered experience of reality and experience psychosis.

Understanding that you are the sum of parts is empowering once you understand how these interact inside you. These parts also interact with other people's parts. When you know about this, you'll start to understand transformational relationships and how interactions can occur that create – or avoid – drama.

Noticing the conflicting parts of you

Let's practically apply this. Think about a goal for your personal life – perhaps to get healthy. One part of you wants to stop eating chips and chocolate. Another part feels entitled to those things.

Let's break it down.

Part: Healthy

- Thinks: *I want to live to 100.*
- Feeling: It loves the feeling of losing weight and having lots of energy.
- Says: 'I know I can do it. Healthy food is worth it.'
- Values: Wellbeing, longevity, how you might look when feeling healthy and energetic.
- Memories: Times when exercising was easy.
- Actions: Base food choices on the impact of what you will feel like in the long run.
- Pictures in your mind: Healthy food, fitting into jeans.
- When moving and walking: Have a spring in your step. Standing tall, confident and smiling.

Now let's think of the unhealthy part.

Part: Unhealthy

- Thought: *I want what I want. It doesn't matter. There's always tomorrow.* May blame other people or situations.
- Values: Feeling good right now.
- Feels: Unsettled, impulsive, righteous and entitled.
- Memories: Comfort food in the past.
- Walking around: Feels a bit like a moody teenager.

Let's explore this now using EI. Using your self-awareness, try this yourself with some conflicting parts of you. You'll know you've got incompatible parts as you may have tried to meet a goal in the past and haven't been able to stick with it. Conflicting parts are often why New Year's resolutions don't last. The parts get in the way of each other.

You might have a goal of talking more with your kids, reducing drinking at night, being less reactive at work, going to bed at a reasonable hour or starting a meditation habit. Start to notice the conflicting parts inside you.

You may find this exercise difficult on your own, even with prompts. That's okay. Do what you can. The trick is to catch yourself in the moment and experience it for yourself. Pick a goal you're trying to reach right now. Pay attention in the moment to your thoughts and feelings, how you feel when you walk around or sit, any memories that come up and any images in your mind.

Another way to do this is to think about a decision you might need to make. Notice how all the different parts of you have a different opinion on the subject. Now you can start to see that all these parts of you often have your best interest at heart. They give you a perspective that could be helpful.

CHOOSING THE PART TO LEAD FROM TO SOLVE PROBLEMS AHEAD OF TIME

Choosing which part of yourself to lead from starts with analysing a situation you're likely to face. You may do this instinctively, but when you do it consciously, you can anticipate problems and then solve them ahead of time. There are five aspects to consider:

- the situation
- the team member/s
- your goal
- yourself
- culture.

Let's take a look at each of these.

The situation

The situation is what's happening around you. You could be facing an emergency. You could be in the office. You could be on a ward round. It's the context. You change your actions depending on the situation. You bring a different part to each situation because you operate in a particular role.

The team member/s

When you're leading, you must know what your team needs. The team member in this situation could be the ward pharmacist, the radiologist, the bed manager, the director of nursing or a junior nurse. You need to alter your behaviour depending on their experience or their role. You need to give different information to the director of nursing than you do to the cleaner who's helping in the unit. (We will discuss how to do this in chapters 4 and 5.) It's not just about who they are, but picking up on cues like noticing their behaviour, their response to you or the situation, or aspects of their personality. That's social awareness.

Your goal

When choosing which part of yourself to lead from, think about your goal. What is the ideal outcome you want to achieve? For example, do you want to inspire? Or teach? Or get a task completed? Is the goal to engage your team? Is the goal to have a better relationship with somebody? Is the goal to manage change? Start a project? Getting clear on your goal is required for planning to be a thinking, intentional leader. The goal may change with each situation and person. Or it can be an overarching goal for the day.

Yourself

Now consider yourself. What resources do you need to bring to this situation? Resources include more information or another person to help. Or inner resources such as your strengths, level of energy, and helpful parts. As you are becoming familiar with your parts, you can name them with characteristics that are useful at work, such as 'respect', 'focused', 'positive' or 'patient'.

Think about self-awareness and how you regulate yourself. For example, did you sleep well? Then think about your experience and your personality. You may be able to name your strengths and tendencies to behave already. We will cover this in more detail in chapters 6 and 7.

Culture

Finally, culture is the ideas, customs and behaviours of where you're working. We're like fish, swimming around in the water.

Fish are unaware of what they are swimming in. Culture includes the unit history and the sum of the personalities in the unit. It is the aggregate of what is and isn't tolerated by the whole.

A clinical leader tried to initiate one-to-one coaching sessions with his leadership team. He asked the team to make an appointment with him in the next two weeks. Only one out of six did. These types of sessions weren't in the culture. Some people found it threatening. So the leader had to take a new approach. He made them conversational and informal, before thinking about introducing the formal sessions again.

* * *

When you consider these five aspects you'll get better patient outcomes because you can think about and solve issues ahead of time. This is one of the many ways in this book that I encourage you to reverse engineer your leadership, starting with the results you want. It's a way of leading forward. When you're in the moment, it can be hard to think about new or novel ways of behaving and reacting. When you're not in the moment, you can plan. These five aspects give you a checklist to make this easier. You may already consider all these aspects without thinking, but making it conscious makes you much more effective and deliberate.

Here is a scenario to consider.

Sharon needed to improve the risk management process in her unit. Her goal was to increase levels of reporting. She decided on training to show the team how to use the reporting form, and highlight its importance and the implications of not reporting. But the unit was no closer to the goal two months after the training.

Sharon hadn't considered the unit culture. The team felt the process was a finger-pointing exercise and thought it opened them up to others reporting on their nursing care. They were scared of some sort of payback. Sharon blamed the team because she thought they weren't taking it seriously. But she also didn't ask questions initially to formulate her plan to meet the goal. Can you see the gaps in her analysis of the situation? She didn't check the assumptions behind her planning. What would you have done, knowing what you know now?

You make complex decisions every day. We're analysing aspects of the decision-making process and giving them words, which will strengthen your confidence and allow you to refine and improve your decisions. We're shifting from system one to system two thinking.

Are you starting to appreciate all the moving parts you need to consider every day with every decision you make? Quick decisions are needed day to day. This is a way to see what you do already through a new frame. It also provides a frame of reference for new learning.

THE LEADERSHIP DASHBOARD

When driving your car you use your dashboard for key data. It has the gauges that show you your fuel, speed, oil, water and temperature status of the vehicle. Modern cars have maps to direct you. As you drive you keep your eye on this data to make sure you don't run into trouble with the car and you are going in the right direction. To revolutionise your leadership you need to become more deliberate. You can create and start filling out a leadership dashboard. It's a guide for what is important. I got the idea of a leadership dashboard from the Center for Executive Coaching.

This is the organisation I did my Health Leadership coaching course through. In business it's equal would be a business plan. At the end of this book, you'll have a complete plan that you can use to develop your dashboard.

Think about some goals you have. A goal might be a particular project. It could be engaging certain staff or increasing delegating tasks. It could be creating a social committee. It could be developing your feedback skills. Whatever they are, write down some of your goals. Then conduct the five-point analysis for each goal:

- **The situation.** Why you want this goal and when the best time will be to implement it. What assumptions do you have about this situation?

- **The team member/s.** What about your key relationships? Who are the people critical to your success and the success of your area of responsibility or this goal? Be sure to consider relationships. Look up, down, across and even outside the organisation. How will you engage with everybody? How will you know you're engaging with them successfully? What are your goals with these critical relationships? What modes of communication will you use and how often? What is your key message?

- **Your goal.** Think about your goal. What is the outcome you want to achieve? Do you want to inspire? Or teach? Or introduce a new system? Is the goal to start a project, or get rid of something that's not working?

- **Yourself.** What resources do you need to bring to this situation? Who else do you need to be to bring this about? What parts of yourself should you bring to this situation?

- **Culture**. Consider the culture in the unit. It could be hard to see it at first, but there are invisible rules at work. What's been the culture in the unit around change, new initiatives or reviewing how you work? Is your general culture parental, adult or childish? A parental culture is controlling and top-down, an adult culture is trusting and empowered, while a childish culture is an immature drama, with politics and game playing. Or is it a combination of all three?

PAT YOURSELF ON THE BACK

Do you hold back on congratulating yourself due to a lack of confidence or comparisons with other leaders? It's common when learning something new to focus on the gap between what you know and what you don't know, rather than the knowledge you have gained so far. Dan Sullivan and Benjamin Hardy describe this phenomenon in the book *The Gap and The Gain*. They state that high-functioning people focus on the gain, and seeing their behaviours in this way is the foundation for their subsequent successes. You can do this with your team as well. Anyone lacking confidence often focuses on the gap rather than the gain. When my clients seek more self-confidence, they often cannot name what they are proud of in their day. Confident people can always list what they did well. Can you list what you are proud of in your day today?

Remind your team of how far they have come. Or the unit has come. But start with *you*. Can you map your learning journey and pat yourself on the back?

CONCLUSION

We have discussed the power of being authentic. But there's also a danger when we listen to our feelings that this can lead to drama and reactivity. You've learned about your parts and an adaptive way to work with them. You've developed a fundamental understanding of the formation of your personality. And you can now start your leadership dashboard with a process to plan and lead forward. Taking in the complex landscape of your role is going to help enormously.

You can start to plan and know who you need to be. Have a person in mind as you fill out your leadership dashboard. You need to stop focusing on what you don't know and start thinking about who you need to be for your goal. An example of who you need to be would be coming from the respectful part of you so you can help your team feel more valued.

We explore in depth what nurses care about in the next chapter – you must understand this to influence them to do great work. Knowing what motivates your team separates leavable from unleavable leaders and supports them to provide excellent nursing care.

4

What nurses care about today

UNDERSTANDING WHAT YOUR TEAM NEEDS

I've rowed surf boats for over a decade and love it! It's nice to be on the water, get a bit of exercise and be with friends. In planning our training strategy, we start with the goal and the type of proposed race. To improve, we can't just turn up and row. Is it a series of 800m sprints? A 25km row across the harbour, a seven-day marathon or a row to the Tiwi Islands? Even though we are 'just rowing' in all of these, there is a different kind of fitness, stroke rate and even new skills required (like practising getting in and out of the boat from the water). Our training strategy arises from the relevant goal, and in each training session we are clear on what we are improving. But if we don't have a specific goal or event coming up and we just go through the motions, our rowing gets sloppy, and this does not win races. Or make us fit. Or improve our technique.

Are you turning up to your shift like I row when I don't have an event on the horizon?

Start each day without a goal in mind and your leadership could be sloppy and ad hoc. Instead, start the day with an engagement strategy. This will set you apart from others and revolutionise your leadership. Know what you must remember to meet your goal for yourself and your team.

Transformational relationships and leadership require you to know what others need so they stay. Inducting and training large numbers of new nurses can be exhausting. I spoke to a nurse leader who was talking about retiring. She felt this fatigue, plus anger. She said if she saw one more shiny new nurse with a perky ponytail, she'd scream. It's hard to know if the stress pushed her over the edge as she retired a few short months later.

Less staff turnover also means you are going to like your job more, and you are going to feel more confident as a leader. Two US hospitals mitigated the risk of burnout and staff leaving by introducing two strategies: cultivating a culture of respect and improving staff development opportunities. We know that 2021 was one of the most challenging years in healthcare, but they managed to maintain high levels of staff engagement. After the initiative, they stated their nurses responded to COVID-19 'with energy and resourcefulness rather than fatigue and despair'.

In 2014, a review of 730 Dutch nurses reported similar engagement findings from a questionnaire exploring what would stop staff from working until retirement. The key reasons for leaving were:

- lack of job satisfaction
- work pressure
- little autonomy
- lack of appreciation

- lack of support from senior management
- poor educational opportunities.

Knowing what your team needs should form the foundation of how you operate. Your goal is for the team to feel committed and enlivened. The natural flow-on effect will be better patient care by a team that goes over and beyond. You will have shifted their focus from extrinsic motivators to intrinsic ones.

One thing that matters in your unit is nurses' sense of agency or autonomy. Stressful situations increase uncertainty and a perceived lack of choice. A loss of control (among other things) increases the risk of burnout and mental health issues. Jianbo Lai et al. (2020) uncovered this risk when they looked at factors associated with mental health outcomes among healthcare workers exposed to the coronavirus in 2019. Improving control means improving empowerment and engagement. For a team to feel that type of control, you will have to hand over some power to them. We will discuss what brings feelings of more power shortly.

Your team's feeling of fulfilment reduces turnover, and they experience a better quality of relationships. If you have an engaged team, you'll be getting great positive feedback from them. You will feel like you're on the right track. Sounds like a fairy tale? We will see. I facilitated a six-month workforce wellbeing program that included leadership development in a prominent inner-city operating theatre. One of the outcomes of the program was daily sick leave was reduced from nine a day to three or four. The leadership team considered the engagement strategies I outline in this book as a critical factor in that remarkable result.

When you are more engaged with your team, they stay around longer. If you've got less turnover, you'll have more nursing staff.

Life is less stressful when you have more staff and you're not scrambling to get the numbers to be safe every shift.

In this chapter, we talk about how, in transformational relationships, we need to understand what the bedside nurses want and need. This chapter is the first of two chapters covering this aspect, which you must consider daily.

Engaging your team members requires you to understand four components and learn the skills needed in each element.

THE SPARK THAT COMES FROM A VISION

Dave Pugh, a dynamic community services leader of Anglicare in the Northern Territory, wanted to know what motivated his team. So he asked what inspired them to get up and come to work. From the 20 values collected, he distilled five core values. The leadership team wove these values into the organisational culture and stories around why the organisation did what it did. Two critical values were kindness and profound respect; he said these mirror how their managers lead, which he says, in turn, is how the team treats their clients.

Having a vision is a contrast to the mindset of just 'making it to each shift and getting through the next eight hours'. Start with having a vision worth following and relaying it to your team. This is leading forward. A shared vision is 'a force in people's hearts, a force of impressive power'.[1] At its most basic level, a shared vision is an answer to the question, 'What do we want to create?'

I don't think many hospitals work from a vision. (Please contact me if I am wrong.) This chapter will describe how I do visioning with groups, from general nurses to leadership teams. Finding out

---

1   Peter Senge, the founding chair of the Society of Organisational Learning, in his book *The Fifth Discipline* described a shared vision this way.

your core values is an integral part of discovering your vision. A fine example of a hospital that works by its values is the Royal Melbourne Hospital. Their values are people first, lead with kindness and excellence together. Those three values create an idea of who you can be and how you can act as you live the vision.

Sometimes you might think your duties are rooted in the day-to-day functioning of the ward, and it's hard to see how working from a vision is helpful. But every day, we inspire our team to see the impact of what we do and how it fits into the bigger picture. Having a vision gets you out of feeling like you're stuck in a system. From the COVID-19 pandemic, we have seen the rapidity of changes in processes that came from aligning behind a big enough 'why'. Many leaders feel like they don't have time to create a vision – rightly so when there is no time off the floor to do so. Those leading from the floor don't feel like the concept comes from them. In contrast, a complaint I hear from nurse unit managers is that the leaders on the floor are not operating from a higher level, and they'd like them to.

I am often not sure they are talking about the same things. The interesting part is there doesn't seem to be a shared language about visioning and the quality of thinking that needs to occur at that higher level.

Creating a strong vision

Sometimes the vision is created by the whole team, but seldom is a unit vision developed by all the staff. With nurses changing wards and hospitals, it can be felt they inherit a culture without a vision. Imagine if everybody came together and talked about what the team most wanted to create in the unit. In a nurse management publication, Cynthia Gregory, in the article 'Creating a Vision for a Nursing Unit', says there are five steps to creating a vision:

1. include everyone
2. get consensus
3. assure congruence
4. get an objective, creative facilitator
5. keep the vision statement visible and energising.

What problem do you want to solve when creating *your* vision? What image do you have of the future? What would you hope to achieve in the next five years if there were no issues around your work? What could be possible? Note your enthusiasm and passion when you ask inspiring questions that take your work from the mundane to the extraordinary. Inspiring questions can bring excitement to the process. To create a vision, flesh out values or create fresh ideas, try brainstorming for questions rather than answers. 'Brainstorming for questions rather than answers makes it easier to push past cognitive biases and venture into uncharted territory,' states the Executive Director of MIT Leadership Center, Hal Gregersen, in *Harvard Business Review*.

A type of vision can be how we frame roles – changing a grievance officer to the minister for peace, or a falls auditor becomes a safe-and-sound officer. A risk-management champion becomes a learning-in-action champion. Take a mundane name and turn it into something inspiring and fun. Inspiration is the fuel that ignites. It motivates you. Motivation, when you break it down, is a motive for action. It's connecting to something higher, broader and deeper than you.

After the great fire of 1666 that levelled London, the world's most famous architect, Christopher Wren, was commissioned to rebuild St Paul's Cathedral. As the story goes, on a day in 1671, Wren observed three bricklayers on a scaffold. One was crouched, one stood slumped, and another stood tall and focused on his work. Wren went up to the crouching bricklayer and asked him what he was doing. The bricklayer said, 'I'm a bricklayer. I'm working, making this wall to feed my family.' The second one who slouched responded to the same question: 'I'm a builder, and I'm making a wall.' The third bricklayer, who was proud and efficient, stated, 'I'm a cathedral builder. I'm building a great cathedral to the glory of God.' Seeing the results and how your work contributes to the vision motivates and can change how you attend to your daily tasks.

A self and social regulation exercise would be to trial talking about how your daily work contributes to the wellbeing of the community and improving your patients' lives. Or connecting yourself and them to that with data. Then notice the energy shift in both you and them.

Leaders are said to lead energy, making this an important exercise to trial. My bet is that you increase your and their engagement. But don't believe me. Try it for yourself.

A visioning exercise I do with a whole unit or a leadership team is an exercise using Lego Serious Play. Organisations such as Google, Samsung, Virgin Atlantic and even the UN use this creative experiential process using Lego. The process involves asking questions to get the mind and hands to create models that represent concepts and ideas instead of tangible things such as houses and cars. A question I ask in the visioning workshop is, 'It's three years into the future, and you have won an award for the best team in reducing turnover and increasing performance. What have you done to win this award?' This line of questioning helps the group to think back from the future and reverse engineer it. The Lego Serious Play process enables creativity and innovation that doesn't get to happen in the day-to-day task-driven unit operations.

Leading from the future is a valuable concept. What would it be like if you started asking, 'What if … ?' or 'Imagine if … ?' Notice what happens in your body. Ask yourself inspiring questions – take a chance and think about what could happen. If you're in charge of a shift, it can feel unrealistic that you could invoke some sort of higher vision in the unit. But if not you, who? Gandhi is thought to have said, 'Be the change you wish to see in the world.' Thinking of being the change could ignite you into action and being who you need to be for your team.

Some nurses may feel that a vision is too conceptual. Thinking it doesn't give direction can lead to role ambiguity and a lack of shared understanding of standards. Engagement, empowerment and working from a vision don't mean you take your hands off the reins of the unit. But they do mean you give the team enough power to stay interested and you allow space to develop themselves. Everyone contributes to the story. To make it practical you can reduce the vision to goals, milestones and tasks, and then schedule it. This process has reduced burnout in a nurse manager that I took through this project management process. She has re-engaged with her work with more energy and is achieving her vision for her area in a way she never thought possible.

In one workshop, a person was excited about an aspect of the vision: recycling. She wanted to make the unit more ecologically friendly. Saving the planet by recycling wasn't a key part of every-one's vision, but the whole team was happy to let her be excited about it. That was her contribution to the ward.

Have a bit of fun with this – list all the names of senior roles in your unit. You can also include projects you might have. Change the names as I did above, like the falls auditor becomes a safe-and-sound officer. I did this with one group, and the 'systems and details'–type people didn't like it, while another group did. Allow people to have a name that feels right for them.

Don't rush forward without giving thought to *what if* ... allow yourself to imagine. Open up conversations with others and see what they have to say about their dreams for your unit or even healthcare as a whole. Empower them to share ownership and ignite their own spark with the excitement of possibilities. Allow space for what could be and let some individual personality enter the ward to transform it for the better.

THE CAMELOT PROMISE

As an adventurous young girl, the legendary story of King Arthur and his knights of the round table inspired me. A place of magic and romance. I felt optimism with the higher characteristics of the King and his knights as they embodied valour, respect, success, love and equality.

I felt I could actualise the 'Camelot promise' after teaching a group of peer supporters active listening. For me, the Camelot promise means that we all can come from a higher place and treat others as equals. And when we do that, something magical unfolds in each person. A skill such as active listening can connect people and help others feel accepted as the listener comes from a place of respect and equality. With the success stories on day two of the peer supporter training, I discovered how groundbreaking active listening and the mindset behind it were for the participants' relationships. The men in the group noticed it was easier to hold back from trying to solve their wife's problems as they used the skills I have outlined in this chapter. Skills such as door openers are the prompts for starting active listening.

Active listening

Active listening is a crucial communication skill for the engagement and feedback processes, which we will discuss in detail in chapter 8. Active listening is a process nurses often think they do well. But when I teach this, it's apparent they don't know how. Active listening is not just listening to what is said but reflecting back through a statement about what you heard. It reflects on the feeling, the values, the content or even body language.

One of my fundamental values is being authentic and talking about important things. Active listening gives the skills to allow someone to sit with real feelings, feel understood and not become caught up in them. Because of this, it remains one of my favourite skills to teach.

Active listening helps you connect nurses to their purpose. When your team has a space to talk, they can think out loud. Sometimes, people learn best by talking. With the generational search for meaning and authenticity, this leadership skill helps them share what is important to them. Having their key drivers heard by you will feel valuable to them. Listening also helps with continuous improvement and shows your team you value them. By actively listening, you're going to gain your team's trust.

What is *not* active listening is the statement, 'I understand what you're saying'. This statement doesn't check understanding or convey effort on behalf of the relationship. When you're listening and taking the time to do it, it's demonstrating to the other person their value and that what they say is important to you. Besides the increase in connection and relationship building, you gather information from the frontline. You are making listening in this way part of continuous improvement.

When coordinating activities in the ward, it is not easy to pause to listen. Remember why listening is the number one engagement and relationship tool, and prove it yourself. Use your self-awareness to take a breath and calm your mind to listen. Your stressed mind can lure you into thinking you have no time; see if you can find just 30 seconds.

Door openers help you encourage the other person to keep talking. Door openers are things like, 'Ah, yes', 'Okay', and, 'Hmm'. They're all the small things to signal, 'Keep going. I see. I'm listening to you,' as well as using an open body posture and good eye contact (if it's culturally appropriate).

Another part of active listening is summarising. You summarise because you want to let the other person know you understand them. But you're also checking to make sure what you heard is correct. You can summarise at the end of your conversation to confirm pertinent details.

Active listening is the best skill a leader can learn to improve team performance, engagement and patient safety. You will be more respected and feel more connected to your team. Have you ever been at a party and sat listening to someone for a long time? You didn't say much, just listening to them, being respectful, and later you heard they liked you? You're thinking, *wow, I didn't share too much of myself.* But what they wanted was the feeling of acceptance, trust and respect.

Allowing your team to talk stimulates the vagus nerve, enabling them to relax. In my leadership training, one-third of all nurse leaders say this active listening skill was one of the best skills they learned. You might already think, *I know how to listen*. Regardless of your current skills – and many of you *are* skilled at this – you can learn to refine your listening.

Some of you may be fearful that you think you have to be a counsellor as well as a nurse. Active listening *is* a counselling skill, but that doesn't mean you are counselling. It's also a leadership coaching skill.

You can pick your time to listen. You can say, 'It sounds like this is important. Is it okay if we talk about this later?' Then make a time that suits you both. Acknowledging the importance of the conversation recognises their value with words and actions. You can also stop the conversation if you think it's gone on for long enough. Summarise what you have heard and then ask them what they would like to do next.

Then you just have to remember to do it!

To make active listening easy, here's a list of reflection starter phrases:

- Could you help me to understand? You mean ... ?
- On the one hand, you ... and on the other hand ...
- Let me get this right ...
- For you, it sounds like ...
- It seems as if ...
- What I hear you saying is ...
- I get a sense that ...
- You see this as ...
- I get the picture that ...
- You are painting the picture of ...
- It looks like ...
- It feels as though ...

- I want to check …
- It's like …
- Is this what you mean?
- I see, for you …

Everybody has a natural way of talking. Pick a sentence starter that feels natural to you and practise using it. Active listening doesn't have to start this way. But this is a guide.

When teaching active listening I deliberately share the skill before I teach coaching questions. This is because question asking is a skill that nurses already have. Listening actively without trying to solve the problem does not come naturally to most nurses. Be sure to practise active listening before you practise the coaching questions listed later in this book.

After learning to listen actively, I have noticed that leaders also often overdo summarising and overdo question asking. Asking a question is not active listening. So watch for that. Active listening can be simple. You don't have to reflect on the whole statement. Sometimes, you can do a part of it. For example, if they say, 'I haven't been sleeping well of late. There's been a lot going on at home, and I'm finding I can't focus well at work.' You could reply, 'A lot is going on for you', or, 'The stress is affecting your focus and sleep', or, 'You're stressed at the moment'.

Can you see there are many ways to do it? Begin by reflecting at least once a day. There will be many opportunities to practise; even if you reflect on one statement in a conversation, that is a good start. Don't take my word that this is the best skill you will learn. Do it and find out for yourself.

A few things get in the way of good listening. Remember to take a breath if you give advice habitually. People don't want advice.

Can you remember the last time you ever followed through on advice? You also might be tempted to jump in when you listen and ask questions to get more information. It can sound like an interrogation or lead the person away from what they think is essential if you ask questions. Don't worry; I will give you some questions you can ask in chapter 7 when I introduce coaching skills.

What if you disagree with what your team are saying and are scared they will think you agree with them while active listening? In my leadership training, participants stated this fear. Look at this example of active listening from Mary, who is trying to understand why Jade is so upset. She listens with curiosity, open to hearing Jade's views without problem-solving.

Jade: I need to talk to you about the tea break cover.

Mary: Sure, come on in.

Jade: Today was the second time this week I was late to get my break. I get ravenous.

Mary: You get really hungry, and it's stressful.

Jade: Yes, and it doesn't seem to stress the access nurse who is supposed to cover me. I get forgotten every time.

Mary: It sounds like you think it's personal.

Jade: Maybe … why does it keep happening to me?

Mary: You're not sure.

Jade: The process should be better.

Mary: So the process is the problem.

Jade: Yes.

And so on. You can see that with active listening, the conversation progresses, and if you stay curious and open, you can get to the bottom of their thoughts, not yours.

COMPASSION AS A LEADERSHIP SUPERPOWER

Research of 15,000 leaders from Project Potential found a correlation between compassion and promotability. Compassion is a win–win strategy that helps your team and helps you. The ambitious nurse can take heart that compassion also increases the chances of promotion. Compassion opens the mind up to ideas and possibilities – an essential skill when the nurse leader's mind is often searching for risks in the ward and in situations, and can have a negative bias. Being able to cultivate compassion at will is an essential skill in understaffed wards, as it's easy and natural to focus on what is missing rather than what could be.

Compassion is a leadership engagement superpower that assists you in leaving the conversation better than you found it. Compassion has four elements:

- **The other:** paying attention to the other person, being present with them and attending to them.
- **Understanding:** through a dialogue with the person, understanding what's causing their suffering.
- **Empathising:** having an empathetic response; hearing the other person's feelings without being overwhelmed.
- **Helping:** having a helping mindset in the conversation.

You will note that all elements of compassion are present in active listening and can be demonstrated in your body language, voice and tone. Michael West, author of *Compassionate Leadership: Sustaining wisdom, humanity and presence in health and social care*, defines compassion as a sensitivity to the suffering in self and others with a commitment to try to alleviate it and prevent it.

Combining compassion with wisdom also lets you know what motivates and engages other people. The combination of compassion and wisdom helps you lead your team forward. Showing compassion to other people increases trust because they feel listened to and supported. As you cultivate compassion, you increase self-awareness and social awareness. Cultivate self-compassion and it increases self-regulation.

Compassion and collaboration go hand in hand. Compassionate leadership in nursing reduces the command-and-control style and increases adaptability.[2] If you remember, I stated in chapter 1 that anxiety has risen in nursing, which increases the risk of burnout. Compassion also helps alleviate stress. Compassion is becoming the aspirin for nurse leaders in many situations.

You might think, *aren't I already compassionate? I'm a nurse, aren't I?* But according to Sofie Baguley, Vinayak Dev, Antonio Fernando and Nathan Consedine (2014), there are four obstacles you can succumb to that get in the way of being compassionate:

- burnout and overload
- working in a bureaucratic system
- difficult patients and families
- complex clinical situations and uncertainty.

---

2   According to Paquita de Zulueta, the clinical leader of the Empirical College Healthcare Trust.

These obstacles to compassion are present in our VUCA world and healthcare environment, making cultivating compassion a worthwhile but tricky goal.

Self-compassion

Embedded in nursing is the nurturing of others. Often you are compassionate to other people, but not to yourself. Cultivating mindfulness and being present can lead to compassion for self and others. The definition of mindfulness from Jon Kabat-Zinn – who is said to have brought mindfulness to the West – is 'paying attention in a particular way on purpose, in the present moment, and nonjudgmentally'. He sometimes adds, 'in the service of self-understanding and wisdom'. Mindfulness is the way to the present moment, and presence is a state of mindfulness.

Kabat-Zinn says mindfulness can disconnect us from drama:

> We all take ourselves too seriously because we believe that there's someone to take seriously. That 'me'. We become the star of our own movie. The story of 'me', starring, of course, me! And everyone else becomes a bit player in our movie. And then we forget that it's a fabrication. It's a construction. And that it's not a movie, and there's no 'you' that you can actually find if you were to peel it back.

He calls this 'selfing', when we are run by the continuous narrative of our mind. Your mind is a wondrous thing, and the parts that remember, compare and contrast and think logically enable us to function. But how do you decide which thoughts you should listen to? Mindfulness gets you into your objective observer's mind and can help you see the forest for the trees to disengage yourself from your inner chatter.

Mindfulness also increases EI and the ability to lead yourself.

Answer these questions:

Self-awareness: What thoughts can you notice? Can you notice that the same thoughts have different intensities at different times?

Self-regulation: Are you aware of when certain thoughts arise and you don't pay attention to them as they are not relevant?

Social awareness: When you are more objective and mindful you will notice that you won't get triggered by others. You will just notice and you won't make a story up in your mind of what they are saying. Can you notice this happening?

Social regulation: When you are more mindful, notice that you calm others down too as you are not reactive and are neutral. You can pivot to what is necessary. Also note that you can shift into listening more and give your team what they need. Can you notice this happening?

How can you cultivate mindfulness? Mindfulness is being present. Instead of thinking about the past or the future, you can bring your attention to the current moment. Be curious and open to the experience without judging it.

One way to become mindful is to close your eyes when you feel comfortable doing so. It is good to try this when you have time to experiment rather than when you are busy. Pay attention to the sounds around you, noticing if any thoughts arise – not engaging in their content, but 'seeing' them. Notice your thoughts like they're a thing or an object. Feel the temperature of the air on your skin.

Become aware of the shape of your body. Let go of any judgemental thought that comes into your mind, but pay attention. Notice your breath going in and out, your belly rising and falling. Be mindful of being in the moment. It's relaxing because you're not paying attention to any stressful thoughts. It's about going to a part of your mind not engaged with worry. You can use a mindfulness app to help you develop your mindfulness skills, such as Headspace, Smiling Mind or Calm – or practise being in your five senses. And I have a fabulous recording on my website called 'Leaf on a Stream' that enables you to get a reasonable distance from your thoughts. It's 14 minutes long.[3]

Not sure if you have noticed, but nurses find it easier to be kinder to others than to themselves. Kristin Neff, a prolific researcher on self-compassion, says to try these three things:

- **Self-kindness instead of judgement:** Understand and be gentle towards yourself. Know you are imperfect rather than criticising yourself.

- **Common humanity instead of aloneness:** Understand you're human, vulnerable and imperfect, and facing what other people face. Often there's a sense of isolation when you're going through a hard time. Be easy on yourself and share yourself with others. You'll see everybody's doing it tough, and you're not alone.

- **Mindfulness:** Get a comfortable distance from your thoughts instead of over-identifying them. Over-identifying is when you give too much attachment to your thoughts. You become swept up in them. They become significant in your mind,

---

3   https://c4consultancy.com.au/resources/

and you don't have a balanced perspective. Mindfulness is a non-judgmental state where your thoughts come and go, and you simply observe them. You don't try to make them go away or make them wrong for being there.

My clients have said these three things created a turning point for them by quieting the mind of criticisms and their confidence has soared. We will discuss presence further in chapter 7, and I'll provide more tips on how I stayed present while working in ED and ICU.

VALUING YOUR TEAM

What you appreciate grows in value. Besides listening to your team, there are five other ways to appreciate them. Through the successful book *The Five Love Languages* by Gary Chapman, you may already be familiar with these. The five love languages have transformed romantic relationships with the knowledge of how we most like to express and receive love. I used the five ways in my counselling practice when young people didn't feel loved by their parents. I was pleased to see Gary Chapman co-wrote another book with Paul White called *The Five Languages of Appreciation in the Workplace*. It mirrors the five love languages, making them easy to remember.

The five ways to value your team are:

· words of affirmation
· quality time
· acts of service
· gifts
· physical touch.

Paul White admits that 'healthcare providers live under the tyranny of the urgent', pointing towards a need for finding quick but meaningful ways of communicating appreciation.

An example of words of affirmation is, 'You did a great job. I'm proud of you.' When you say it in front of other people, it's even more valuable.

Quality time could be listening and asking people how they are. It's about spending time with somebody. One suggestion from Paul White is for nurse leaders to come in on night duty, or leave the team a thank you note.

The act of service is asking, 'How can I help you?' It might be making them a cup of tea or coffee, doing a job for them or filling in a chart.

A gift could be a small gesture as a present. One of the girls I worked with would make little potted herbs and leave them for her workmates in the tearoom.

You have to be careful with physical touch for obvious reasons, but it could be a high five, a pat on the back or an arm rub. I would only do this with those I thought would be open to it and if it felt authentic.

APPRECIATING YOUR TEAM

Remember, your team is knowledgeable. Nurses have gone to university. Asking their opinion shows you value them. Check if they want your advice before you give it. Remember Mary and Jade and the active listening example: Jade does want a result but also wants her manager to know it was hard for her. A nurse unit manager I was coaching found that asking her team their opinion was the quickest fix to get engagement. She couldn't believe it was so simple to get them on board with a change initiative to improve quality and standards.

Giving them opportunities to grow and develop is a way to value your team – including encouraging professional development. If you appreciate them, they will want to keep performing at a high level and show you how valuable they are.

When nurses' knowledge is appreciated, they suffer less burnout, relationships in the team flourish and performance flourishes.[4]

'I appreciate my team already,' is what 69% of leaders say. Paul White says there's a mismatch between the leaders who appreciate their team and those who said they felt it. The way leaders are showing appreciation isn't received as that. To get appreciation right, you must look at what your team appreciates. Are they verbal in their gratitude to others? If so, give them words of affirmation. Do they make tea and coffee for their teammates? Or do they leave gifts for others? You can match that appreciation once you know what they prefer. Then you will be speaking a language they understand.

Some nurses think their team shouldn't need appreciation for doing their job. But a little appreciation goes a long way, and everyone loves to feel seen for what they are doing.

My language of appreciation in the workforce is words of affirmation and acts of service. A workmate once told me I was too optimistic and used words of affirmation too often, and it came across as insincere. Ouch! Good feedback, though.

---

4   We have seen this in a 2007 study by Valarie Yeager and Janna Wisniewski on nurse retention. And a 2020 meta-analysis of 10 papers exploring the retention of community nurses revealed three critical reasons for leaving: work pressure, work conditions and a lack of manager appreciation. This was by Edwin Chamanga, Judith Dyson, Jennifer Loke and Eamonn McKeown, named 'Factors Influencing the Recruitment and Retention of Registered Nurses in Adult Community Nursing Services: An integrative literature review'.

Words seem cheap to some people – they want action. And we must be careful about physical touch and ensure we have the type of relationship to do a high five or pat somebody on the back. Whatever you do, ensure it is genuine.

Don't use the language of appreciation as a quick fix. It will fall on deaf ears in really stressful and uncertain times. When things are difficult, simply listening is a far better strategy, or spending time getting the resources needed. Task-focused behaviour is better than relational. This may only be for a certain amount of time on bad shifts. Don't stay in a transactional style for too long. (You will see why in the next chapter.)

HAVING HIGH EXPECTATIONS OF YOUR TEAM

One of the most discussed behavioural studies is an experiment named the 'Oak School Experiment', conducted by Harvard psychologist Robert Rosenthal. The experimenters told the teachers the students they were teaching were brilliant, despite their poor grades. The teachers' high expectations of the children increased their academic performance significantly. This experiment demonstrated that having high expectations about others' capabilities creates unconscious cues. These communicate to others your expectations of their behaviour. Then their behaviour rises to the occasion, and they perform better. (This is known as the Pygmalion effect.)

Has this ever happened to you? When another saw more in you than you could, and it drove you to your full potential? Imagine your team as a group of nurse superstars. Talk about them to others like that and watch them swell to meet your expectations. A director of nursing wanted to create change in the hospital. The initiative didn't go through with some wards, as a nurse unit manager introduced the change with, 'I know you are busy enough without these changes but executive want this to go through'. She implied that she wasn't on board with the change and she saw her team as stretched already and unable to enact the new protocol. She thought she was empathising with her team but she wasn't seeing them as the capable nurses who could change if the 'why' was important enough.

You can influence your team's growth, confidence and engagement by seeing the best in them. Be intentional each day – engage your team and talk to them. A nurse leader I'm working with has a goal to have a good conversation with three of her team daily. Another idea is to pick a team member you don't know well and see if you can find their language of appreciation. Remember not to rely on your default dialect.

If you're finding it hard to appreciate a specific person, search for a shared value that can even increase their chance of likability. Remember the Pygmalion effect and look for their strengths, praise them (genuinely) in front of your team or spend time with them. Remember, you are the head of the tribe. By spending time with them, you can increase their perceived value.

CONCLUSION

Using these engagement skills, you'll become a magnet for committed nurse superstars who won't want to leave. They'll know they are heard and feel you are a safe, empathetic leader. You'll learn how to appreciate them so they feel seen and valued. You will also know how to adjust your style to be what they need, not what's easiest for you.

Stop thinking leadership is so complex that you can't do it. Break it down into small interactions with your team. You can start thinking about acting on this today. Before each shift, remind yourself about which engagement strategy you will practise. You can begin practising listening with your family at home.

In chapter 5, you'll discover the drama-creating nurse identities that are in all of us. You are continuing your knowledge about others and what they need to feel engaged and fulfilled.

5

Your team needs you to be more lion

UNDERSTANDING INTERACTIONS

Marketers and business owners know what their ideal clients want and need. If they don't, they go hungry. 'You will get all you want in life, if you help enough people get what they want.' This famous quote is from sales and motivational trainer and author Zig Ziglar from his book *See you at the Top*. He was a firm believer that if you solve people's problems, you'll be a successful salesperson. He advocated doing whatever it took to find out what they needed and wanted. Put yourself in their shoes, ask them via interview or survey them. Many consultants, like myself, devise training programs around surveys from the nurses on the floor. I then train the leadership team to give the nurses what they want. You will revolutionise your leadership and you will be the nurse leader needed in these times if you know what they want and need and give it to them.

Engagement is one aspect of their work that is important to them. Engagement is more likely to occur when you are not involved with interpersonal power games. In this chapter, I'm going to introduce a high-level understanding of the interactions between people so you can master transformational relationships and be a leader worth following. This elevated perspective is how you go from understanding nurses in a general way to understanding them more specifically. It is then you know how to respond as a leader.

The Oxford Dictionary defines interactions as two things affecting one another. In *Leadership: Enhancing the lessons of experience*, Richard Hughes, Robert Ginnett and Gordon Curphy write that leadership is about the interaction between the leader, the followers and the situation. They say you must understand exchanges so you can alter your behaviour. If you don't have followers, can you be a leader?

In chapter 2, we examined how, as a leader, you can trigger your team's stress response more than anybody else. Dr David Rock, founder of the NeuroLeadership Institute and global organisational consultant, turned to neuroscience to discover what stresses the brain in the workplace. He created the SCARF model, a lens through which humans perceive a threat or reward.

This eagle's eye view or knowledge of interactions is like understanding the interactions between the drugs you might mix. You can get away with basic knowledge when you're a junior nurse, but you need to know more as a senior. This knowledge of interactions will stop you from triggering a potential threat, or it can give you the ability to understand what your team would consider motivating. And it's not just pizza!

Reward responses boost engagement. This is what allows your team to work with intrinsic motivation. Knowing about interactions, you can predict what may go wrong, name it and adjust. To be unleavable and transformational, you need to think about being proactive around relationships.

Do you remember the volcano science experiments you used to do as a child, where you mixed baking soda and vinegar? On their own, they were inert, but when mixed, something extraordinary and messy happened. That's an interaction. Once you know the properties of your interaction, you can make sure these will work for you – not against you.

Now you have a fundamental understanding of the forming of your personality. In this chapter, you'll soon see the utility of the parts of your character in a model of interrelationships with others. You will get to appreciate this model from a neuroscience and a social dynamic perspective.

Your personality determines how you relate to yourself and the world. It is the interface. The formation of the pleaser and the boundary setter was presented in chapter 4. Now I'm going to provide more structure to help you understand power differentials better and further your comprehension of why you and others act the way you do. The system we will be examining combines two theories: Transactional Analysis and the Drama Triangle. Don't worry about the theory names too much. I will help make these more accessible to you when I give them nursing identities. Then we will make them transformational.

TRANSACTIONAL ANALYSIS

Transactional Analysis is an example of social psychology, created by psychoanalyst Eric Berne in the 1950s to analyse the processes of communication. Each communication statement was called, by Berne, a 'transaction'. This model will be the game changer in your nursing leadership journey. I promise.

In Transactional Analysis (TA), there are three 'modes': parent, adult and child. Till now, we have been talking about parts of you. Modes are just a collection of parts. The image below shows parent mode, which has two parts that will be relevant for our understanding: 'critical parent' and 'nurturing parent'. The transactional analysis model is a two-person model as it is an interaction model.

The Transactional Analysis modes

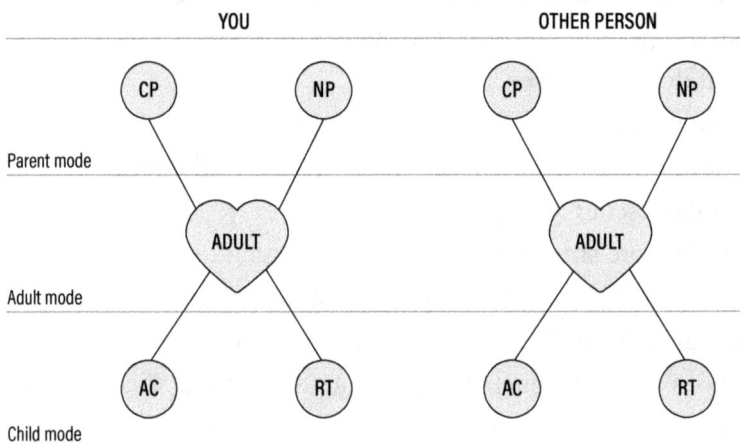

In TA, Berne proposes that a child learns to survive in the world from the examples of adults. You explored your leadership behaviour through this model when you 'located yourself' in chapter 2. TA is the perfect model to consider the power dynamics that both leaders and followers get stuck in.

Parent mode

Parent mode describes some parts of our behaviour and thinking patterns taught by parents, coaches, teachers and other authority figures. The two parts inside this parent mode are the 'critical parent' and 'nurturing parent'.

The critical parent thinks about others: *I have the power. I know more than you.* If there's a conflict, they think: *I win. You lose.* They might think: *I'm okay, but you are not okay. There is something that's missing in you.*

The nurturing parent also thinks: *I have the power. I know more than you.* In a conflict: *I win, you lose.* They also think: *I'm okay. You are not okay.* The difference with the nurturing parent is they want to save others or be the hero. The nurturing parent is overly caring, whereas the critical parent is just how it sounds: critical.

Child mode

The child parts are in action when you think, feel and act like a child. The two child parts we will look at are the 'adapted child' and the 'rebellious teenager'.

The adapted child is the opposite of the critical parent. They don't feel like they have power. They think the other person has the knowledge, and they don't. In conflict: *I lose, you win – and I am not okay, you are okay.* In an adult, this behaviour is victim-like and avoidant.

Then there are rebellious teenagers. You can pick them at 20 paces – eye-rolling, backstabbing and door slamming. Generally, those people are complaining and criticising, trying to take others down while not feeling good about themselves.

Adult mode

Remember, system two thinking is slower and more reflective. Adult mode is how you choose to think, feel and behave as you learn about the world and choose your values. Adult mode is more of a system for thinking – it's logical and slow to make judgments, and this part operates in the present, not the past. In this mode, you are not triggered and stay in a neutral, mindful place. If you're in adult mode, you think power is equal between you and the other, and you consider knowledge equal. With any conflict, this mode goes for win–win, and any interaction has a lack of judgement about the other. There is mutual respect: *I'm okay, and you are okay*. The two key skills in adult mode are assertiveness and listening, both required for a win–win mindset in a conflict.

THE DRAMA TRIANGLE

Now that you have the fundamentals of TA under your belt, I want to introduce you to the other model we need to explore: the Drama Triangle by Dr Steven Karpman. He was a pioneer in distinguishing the parts of self that cause interpersonal drama. Like Transactional Analysis, this is a psychological interaction model, but it describes communication and behaviour from a dysfunctional perspective. He named the three parts 'rescuer', 'prosecutor' and 'victim'.

We have already examined how these parts get developed: via the interaction of your DNA and your experiences with the people around you. For ease, I will place these Drama Triangle parts in parent, adult and child mode below. The rescuer aligns with the nurturing parent. The victim aligns with the adapted child, and the persecutor can align with the critical parent and the rebellious teenager.

Karpman notes that nurses, doctors and anyone else in the caring industry could be drawn to their profession as they see themselves in the nurturing parent/rescuer role.

Transactional Analysis modes and the Drama Triangle

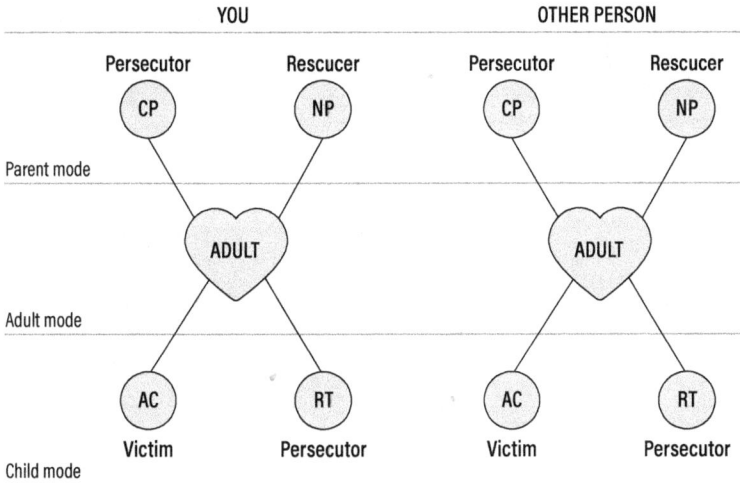

BONDING PATTERNS

Let's look at something we call a 'bonding pattern'. A bonding pattern describes a situation you have been in with another person many times before. It's your pattern of reacting to a certain trigger.

If you have a manager speaking to you in critical parent mode and criticising you, you may automatically meet them as a listener in child mode – either the adapted child or the rebellious teenager. You can't help it because it's a bonding pattern – an unconscious pattern from your past with another authority figure.

If you go to the adapted child, you may blame yourself, be apologetic, and feel upset and maybe teary.

Critical parent to adapted child bonding pattern

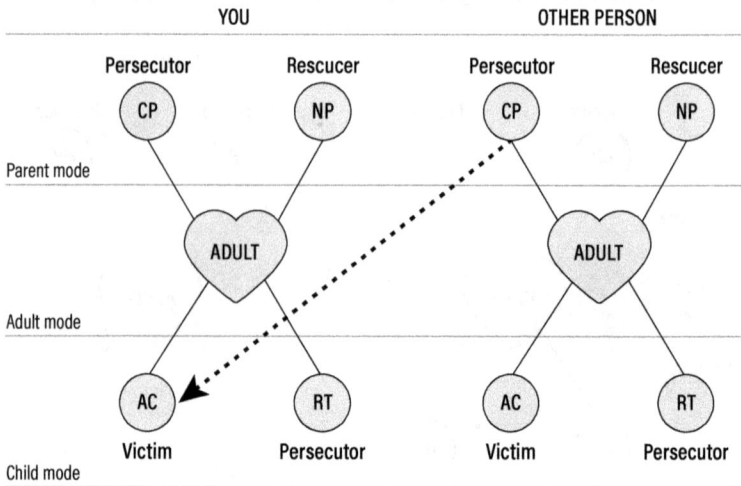

	YOU		OTHER PERSON	
	Persecutor	Rescucer	Persecutor	Rescucer
	CP	NP	CP	NP
Parent mode				
	ADULT		ADULT	
Adult mode				
	AC	RT	AC	RT
	Victim	Persecutor	Victim	Persecutor
Child mode				

Or if you communicate as a rebellious teenager, you might be snarky, 'backstabbing' your leader, and you're caught in a ping pong match with both of you responding critically. The rebellious teen will take the criticism away from the face-to-face interaction and will then complain about you behind your back.

However, once you realise what's happening, you can come into adult mode and decide to respond to the critical part of the communication. You drop the judgement and become proactive.

Responding in a bonding pattern is system one thinking, the energy-saving response – a well-worn path from past behaviours. It is also more likely when you are stressed. (When you are feeling stress you will be in one of the parent modes or one of the child modes. Knowing this means you realise how important emotional self-awareness and self-regulation are.) You don't realise you have a choice about how to respond. Be kind to yourself, as the bonding pattern happens automatically. With increased self-awareness, you can choose to respond rather than react by shifting to adult mode. We will discuss how to do this further in chapters 6 and 7.

Dropping judgement and shifting to adult mode

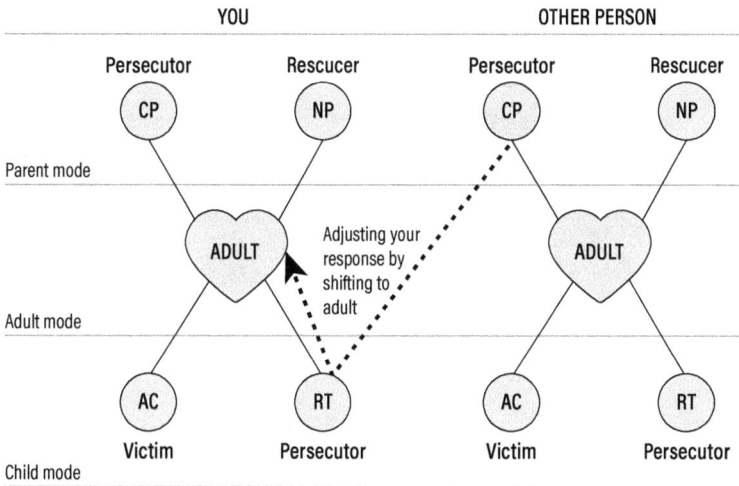

YOU				OTHER PERSON		
Persecutor	Rescucer			Persecutor		Rescucer
CP	NP			CP		NP

Parent mode

ADULT — Adjusting your response by shifting to adult — ADULT

Adult mode

AC	RT			AC		RT
Victim	Persecutor			Victim		Persecutor

Child mode

It's more likely your team will shift into adult mode when you are in adult mode. This particular bonding pattern is the power of being an adult. Imagine your team interacting in a balanced and calm way. Acting professionally, listening, but also being assertive about what they need. No game playing and no second-guessing from anyone.

This adult mode is also where your team learns and performs their best. It's in the middle zone of Yerkes Dodson law you were introduced to in chapter 2. Unlike the parent mode when the individual takes on more responsibility and power and their stress response is turned on.

Adult bonding pattern

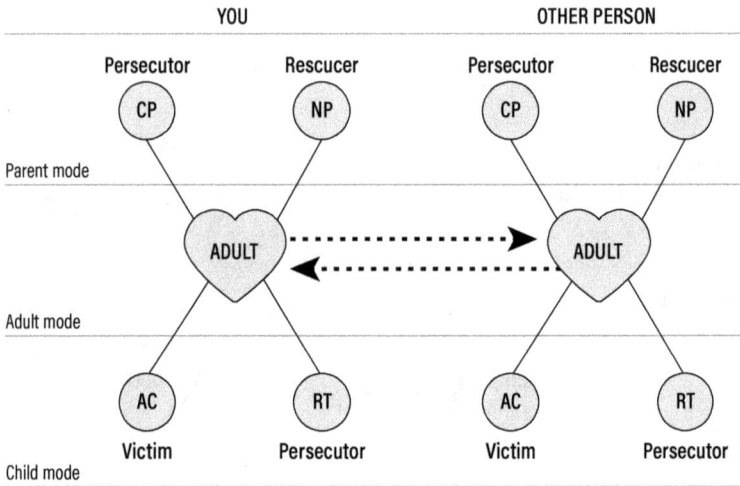

You might finger point at another's behaviour; you think it is out of your control. And it is. But you can and do influence it. One of the most important ways you affect it is with bonding patterns. If you are in adult mode, being respectful, accepting them equally, listening but being assertive and going for win–win, they are more likely to stay! They are more likely to be in adult mode themselves, and the ward will be more efficient, make fewer mistakes, and have less dysfunction. You will *love* your work, and so will they.

It is important not to stay in parent mode. Parent mode means using power to get what you want, you think you are right and try to get your way all the time (a win–lose attitude). Can you see the similarities between the critical parent mode and the autocratic leadership styles? The following statement from Karpman is important for leaders to grasp: 'Win–lose always turns into lose–lose. A win is always temporary.' Think about it. If somebody comes to you and starts complaining, they might be in critical parent or even rebellious teenager mode. Both of those complain. You may go into nurturing parent/rescuer as you try to solve the problem and take it off their hands. Or you match their style of interaction as you become defensive. The biggest thing to note with these transactions is they rob you of thinking and responding from your logical brain and keep the drama going in the ward. More drama, less patient care. Your team stops being engaged; they might take sick leave and could quit.

Your team needs you to be in adult mode, so it's essential to understand these reactions. This combined model I've created gives an idea of how communication goes wrong – learning about it can show you how to manage and change your relationships.

When working as a psychologist, first-time mothers would often book an appointment with me after having their baby. You can imagine how they prepared for the baby. They got the apps and they read the books.

Their husband returns to work after the baby is born, and the mother becomes the family expert on the child. The husband comes home at the end of the day, and she instructs him on how to bathe, feed and hold the baby. As the mother is at home more, she also places herself as the expert on the house – how to hang the washing, dry the dishes, and the like.

The mothers would complain to me: 'I have a baby-baby. I also have a husband-baby. I need to tell my husband what to do. He sits watching television or playing video games. I have to tell him when to take the rubbish out and wash the dishes. I need to give him constant instructions.' Can you see what has happened in these relationships? They are stuck in a bonding pattern. The mother hasn't realised she's in parent mode and put her husband in child mode. The husband becomes this helpless, adapted child who doesn't know what to do and needs instructions all the time. At times he will adopt complaining, teenager behaviour. The dynamic changes when the mother allows her partner to make his own mistakes. And it does change quickly; I've witnessed this marriage-saving shift many times.

Nurse leaders can inadvertently create this parent–child dynamic by over-instructing and always being the 'expert'. They keep their team in child mode, and the team becomes unwilling to step up and take responsibility.

Over directing leads to lack of responsibility

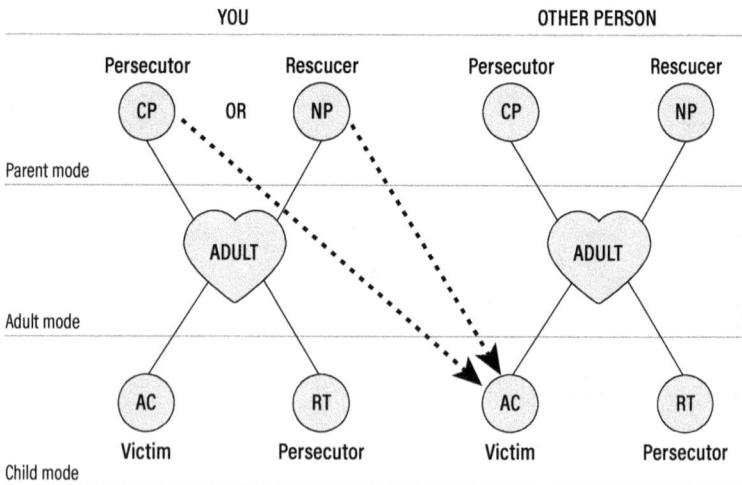

Another complaint from women is their husbands try to solve their problems rather than just listening. The husband advises her, which she doesn't want. She just wants to be heard. She wants an adult-to-adult interaction, and he goes into critical parent with all the answers.

Clients of mine find learning the Transactional Analysis and Drama Triangle model is a big a-ha moment. There's always some vulnerable sharing and cringing at admitting to dysfunctional behaviours. In some heterosexual couples I've seen, the female wants to solve the problems for the male. I've also noticed this pattern in same-sex couples. It's an interaction effect, and it occurs whenever there are humans around. Some might say it doesn't happen in their relationship. If not, congratulations!

There can be confusion when thinking about adult mode and having equal knowledge when dealing with a junior nurse. The way to think of it is that you have the expertise, and they have different abilities. This difference might be knowledge about themselves, the patients they have looked after that day or even personal experience of dealing with a situation. Have an open mind and be open that they hold wisdom and intelligence.

Sometimes you must be in parent mode, give directions and take the lead without listening to others – the old command-and-control model. However, in the long run, this mode leads to others becoming comfortable with you doing this. Then they're going to hand all responsibility to you, and you will be stuck making decisions for them. In chapter 7, I will show you how to give directions without being in command-and-control mode using my Transformational Nurse Identities model.

Do you have teenage girls? What happens when you tell them what to do? They often rebel. One interaction effect is that sometimes mothers start becoming rebellious teenagers as well, fighting with their children like they're both teens. This dynamic can happen at work with nurses engaging in tit-for-tat behaviour.

> Reflect on:
>
> **Self-awareness and regulation time:** Take note of your relationships where the interaction is not easy and you do not listen well to each other. Some people have tried and say, 'I've noticed what's been happening, but I can't shift into another mode.' For now, try taking a breath and name what is happening. This seemingly small action takes you to a non-reactive part of your brain and is a good step towards getting you into adult mode.

Once you come from adult mode more in your interactions, you will notice that others shift into adult mode as well. However, you being in adult mode doesn't guarantee they will match – it just increases the likelihood. Adapted child, rebellious teen, critical parent or nurturing parent could be their default personality. Karpman says some roles can be a 'comfortable life habit' for a person.

NURSE IDENTITIES

Now that you're beginning to understand the different identities we all use and how they affect our work, let's adapt the parts we've just examined – critical parent, nurturing parent, adult, adapted child and rebellious teenager – to the nursing environment. They will now be called 'nurse identities'. The adult is a transformational nurse identity, and the rest are dysfunctional nurse identities. The dysfunctional nurse identities are unstable. They're not satisfying, and they're emotionally competitive. The dysfunctional nurse identities create drama, get in the way of having an engaged team, and make you a leavable leader. With awareness, you can get into adult mode consistently.

I created the nurse identities to make it easy for you to think about them in terms of work. You can go from part to part (identity to identity) with ease. I have used the words 'parts' and 'identities' interchangeably throughout this book. I've named these nurse identities after animals which may feel a bit silly but makes them more memorable – let's have some fun.

In 1996 in Australia, the Board of Works ran a campaign to conserve water due to drought. It was called Don't Be a Wally With Water and featured a cartoon Wally as well as an actor playing Wally on TV. When visiting my family in Melbourne during this time, my mum would remind me not to be a Wally. There was a bucket in the shower to catch the water to be later used for the garden. There was also Norm in the Life Be In It campaign. The character of Norm sat on a recliner with a pot belly, drinking beer. He didn't exercise. No one wanted to be Norm.

This is my goal with merging the nurse identities with animals. You can call yourself and others out on them and it feels less personal and you can take yourself and others more lightly.

Cockatoo

When I think of the critical parent nurse identity, I think of a cockatoo. Bossy, busy, very serious and noisy. Consider the matron of yesteryear, running her critical eye over everything. And you wouldn't want to cross her – she'll screech right back at you. If you are operating in this nursing identity, every task feels very urgent.

You may feel threatened and pressured, and you want to get every-thing right. It feels like your reputation is on the line. You think other people are the weak link, and you don't care how they feel about it. It has to get done – now! A cocky comes to any discussion thinking their way is the best way, so are closed off to any other options. The cockatoo can be quick to anger and get on their 'high horse' of righteousness.

Mumma bear

Now meet the nurturing parent identity, mumma bear (or pappa bear). In the Drama Triangle, Karpman calls this the rescuer. Mumma bear loves to help and has open arms (and paws) to embrace saving everyone! Mumma bears are competent nurse leaders but are burdened with taking on saving everyone. Mumma bears are overly caring. They say, 'I feel for you, and I'll do that for you.' They say, 'I'm responsible for it all. They can't manage. I'm carrying everyone. I always have to work so hard.' If you are in mumma bear identity, you have bought into the hero story of nurs-ing. You might be doing too much for others during work hours and in your personal life. You might even be a people pleaser, and you like to be 'nice'. Mumma bears can also tend to think everyone needs to be like them, and then shift to another nurse identity due to judgement (the lamb, coming up next, or the hyena, closely fol-lowing behind).

Lamb

When I think of the adaptive child part, I think of a lamb. It feels fearful, small, alone, self-pitying and not enough. It's victim-like. It asks the question, 'Why does this always happen to me? What's the use?' It says, 'It's all too much. There isn't enough time. Others can do it, but I can't think of what to do. The system doesn't allow it to happen.'

If you are in this nurse identity, you will focus on problems, not solutions. You will feel trapped in your role – and your life. It feels too big, so you don't try.

Hyena

Now meet hyena, the rebellious teen part. The hyena is a sneaky, back-biting, defensive and blaming nursing identity. The hyena delights in looking for faults, thinks others are the problem, and says, 'It's not fair'. You are in hyena mode as a leader when you blame members of your team or your managers for difficulties. You feel helpless like the lamb, and can often shift to the lamb with a feeling of not being enough. The thought of not feeling enough could be hidden from you but is easy to see when you are defensive. Why be defensive if you have nothing to defend? Hyenas talk behind others' backs instead of taking any responsibility, and they walk around with a sour look on their face.

Lion

Lastly, meet the lion, the adult part and the first transformational nurse identity you get to meet. It's easy to see why a lion is a perfect transformational nurse identity. Composed, fair, conserves energy, walks lightly with quiet confidence, poise and purpose. Lions are totally present. They don't waste time with drama, and they are comfortable making decisions and creating and holding a vision that others can't see yet. Lions respect themselves, and they respect others as well. Lions are the true rulers as they have considered boundaries on behaviour and stay balanced at all times.

BONDING PATTERNS AND NURSING IDENTITIES COMBINED

The diagram below shows how the nurse identities combine with the transformational analysis.

Dysfunctional and transformational nurse identities

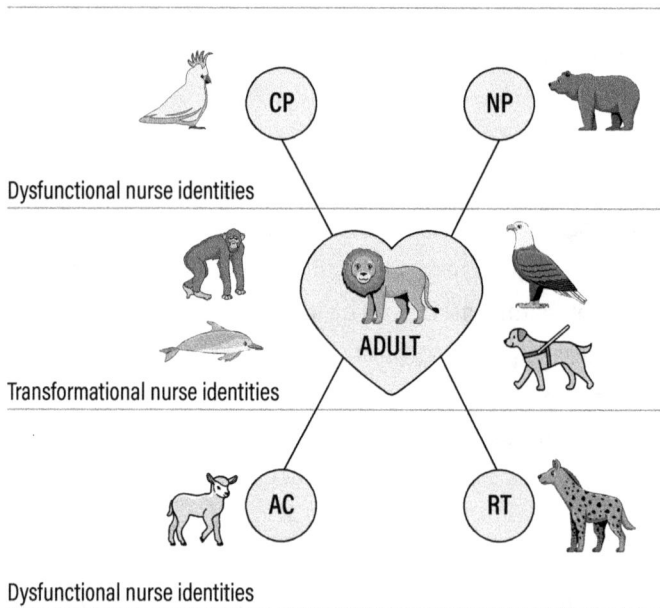

Dysfunctional nurse identities

Transformational nurse identities

Dysfunctional nurse identities

NAVIGATING THE ZOO OF THE UNIT

Now let's see bonding patterns at work using the nurse identities. Imagine you've got a ward of junior lambs. With the cocky as your leader, it's terrible for succession planning because everybody just gets told what to do, the lambs don't learn critical thinking skills, and nobody takes responsibility when a leader is not around.

There's no intrinsic motivation, and the lambs aren't in the habit of thinking for themselves.

The same happens when mumma bear is on for the shift, acting as the nurturing parent, thinking all the juniors aren't capable and doing everything for them – giving them a fish rather than teaching them how to fish.

These interactions happen every day, all around you, and you also flip from one identity to another without knowing it. The critical point to recognise is that you aren't just one nurse identity; you can change from moment to moment. Recognition is the first step in changing something that could be harmful to your team.

I am president of a Surf Life Saving Club, and on Friday nights you'll often find me on the club deck overlooking the beach having an end-of-week drink. When new to the role, wanting to do well by the members, I was listening to their complaints, wanting to fix things – totally in mumma bear mode! Until one night the lamb and hyena some members triggered my hyena, and I left in anger (maybe even with a little tantrum, if I'm honest), blaming them for wrecking my night at the club. I then shifted into thinking as a lamb: *I can't even socialise here now. They have wrecked my downtime.* Once home, I laughed and said, 'Hello, mumma bear, hyena and lamb', when I realised I had jumped from one to another for the last half hour. Even though I had that chuckle to myself once self-awareness kicked in, it took some time to get calm again. I had whipped myself up into a proper state. Naming these identities helped, as I could see the interaction as an age-old drama. I anticipated this dance the following Friday and stayed in lion mode all evening.

We can also use the nurse identities when understanding culture in the unit. We have considered culture using parent, adult or child mode in the leadership dashboard. View culture now employing the nurse identities. Is your culture more lion, cockatoo, hyena or lamb? You might even like to make up an animal name for this yourself. One client of mine called their situation a snake pit, another called a staff member a bull, and another labelled somebody fairy floss as they had their head in the clouds (not an animal, but you can't argue with imagination!). Knowing the culture in your unit allows you to expect the interactions that will occur, anticipate your bonding pattern in response, and then you can plan how to stay in lion.

The parts you've developed all have a purpose. Being the hyena at times is helpful to show you there might be unfairness happening. But after the initial burst of anger, you don't need the hyena anymore. You can say, 'Thanks, I can take it from here', as you slip into lion and deal with the situation. You slip in and out of these identities every day. Being triggered is human. With insight, you can notice they are part of you, and you can change. That's a personal evolution which contributes to the revolution in nursing leadership.

Expect, notice and name

Expect, notice and name the bonding patterns and identities with curiosity and openness. We are all humans who have habitual behaviours. Noticing the patterns in others is easier in the beginning. Name the nurse identities in them without judgement. Then do the same for you.

You can be the cocky to give an instruction and then realise you can do it from lion mode. It might seem stupid to provide yourself with an animal name, but it can soften thinking about yourself in this way, especially when you are in an ineffective, dysfunctional nursing identity. Remember, this is the beginning. You're getting to know these nurse identities inside you and in other people. They are not all of you. They are just a way you have learnt to react and respond to people and situations. They are a way you respond when you are stressed. You'll learn specific ways to get out of these reactive paths in chapters 6 and 7.

Picking up on cues

As a leader you are looking for cues so you can assist others and for self-awareness. Noticing how your team responds to what you say helps you adapt quickly. To do this, you just need to pay attention to their cues – their facial expressions and behaviour. Perhaps even when they are taking sick leave. How another responds to you is a cue to how they are feeling and what they are thinking. This can give you information about your behaviour as they may be responding to you. Or it may not be about you at all.

To determine what the unit feels as a whole, survey them (but make sure you action what you find to keep trust with your team). Picking up on cues, no matter where they come from, is an essential part of emotional intelligence. It's the social awareness aspect, so you can help them regulate their emotions and behaviour. Picking up on cues will help you pivot and change direction in your leadership behaviour.

Naming your and another's emotions helps you regulate your stress. Matthew Lieberman, a scientist at UCLA, conducted a study in 2005 with some groundbreaking results around labelling another person's emotions. He asked 30 participants to view pictures of angry, happy and scared faces. Half the participants tried to match the target face to another face with a similar expression. The other half tried to match the face with a word that correctly labelled the person's feelings. Functional MRI scans of the brain picked up that less activity occurred in the amygdala when people labelled the emotions with words. The amygdala triggers the fear and stress response. When you label feelings with words, you turn off your stress response.

There is a minority of people who will never be happy. Trying to please them is mission impossible, and it's easy to take it personally. Check in with others if you have a difficult person on your team and swap notes to get another perspective.

If you don't know what's happening with a person, don't assume – just ask them. For example, if you notice a shift in someone's facial expressions, check in with them straight away. Ask them how they feel. Ask them what they think. Picking up on cues is information. What you do with the information is up to you. You close the loop in your own brain when you ask a clarifying question, and you can stop wondering and focus on what is essential.

If you've been speaking to another person and notice they weren't happy with what you said, it's okay if you circle back later and say, 'I noticed you may not have been happy with what I said.' Then listen. Your team will appreciate it.

After picking up a cue from a facial expression, it can feel strange to enquire about what someone thinks. But your team members will feel more valued if you do and feel more related to you. I reveal the importance of this below with evidence from neuroscience.

The social brain

Your mind is always surveying the environment for cues. Neuroscientist Evian Gorgon refers to this process as 'the fundamental organising principle of the brain', to move towards what one finds rewarding and away from a possible threat.

These responses are biologically programmed, as cues in our social world affect our survival. Dr David Rock expands on three concepts in 'Managing with the Brain in Mind', a special report from strategy+business. The first is that the brain registers and treats social rewards and threats as physical rewards and dangers. So a social threat at work can feel the same as a threat to our life. Secondly, the threat response is more salient and intense than the reward response. Finally, your team's ability to focus, work, make decisions, solve problems and act collaboratively is reduced when there's a threat response. The good news is the opposite is also true: the reward response increases your team's ability to take necessary actions.

Transformational leaders know how to encourage participation in projects. You discover what will make your team oppose or support your projects by getting familiar with the SCARF model developed by Dr David Rock. The SCARF model outlines five social drivers that your mind scans the environment for. SCARF stands for:

- **S is status or significance:** Status is when a person feels appreciated and their work is valued. They're looking for *I am important compared to others*, which includes feeling respected. Or they are looking for a threat to their status, such as the promotion of someone they think they are more skilled than.

- **C is certainty**, which is being aware of what happens next: We don't always like surprises and new situations. We prefer things mapped out.

- **A is Autonomy:** People like choices, a sense of control and a say in what happens, even if it's just a choice between two options. Otherwise, they feel trapped. Having a choice gives them a sense of certainty as well. It is micromanaging and excessive directing that triggers this stress response.

- **R is relatedness**, a sense of connection to others: Do we have things in common? Are we in the same group? People will get stressed if they feel disconnected from the team; for example, in isolation with a patient for too long or put on a project alone. They feel safe when they know and like others in their team.

- **F is fairness** – a strong response, whether it's for us or others: We can handle a lot if the process seems fair. Your mind prefers a fair reward that could give a small benefit to a significant benefit with an unfair exchange.

These five social triggers are global, but each person is motivated by different drivers or threats. For example, consider entrepreneurs. They're motivated by autonomy and status and handle more uncertainty. An accountant may be more motivated by certainty, and a social worker might be more motivated by relatedness and fairness. What do you think would motivate nurses? My guess is relatedness is number one and then perhaps status (they are a thinking team, after all). During COVID, nurses' fairness was triggered with having to isolate patients from their families.

Building relatedness with your team is imperative. If a team member doesn't feel connected to you, they won't feel much empathy for you. They are motivated to see people they like win and those they don't like fail. You use different brain networks when you feel related to someone. Developing relatedness with your team builds psychological safety. In nursing, there are many cliques. Chapter 6 discusses the good and bad effects of solid friendship groups.

This SCARF model helps make sense of your social interactions at work and enables you to build psychological safety for others. By looking through this lens at your team, you'll be able to understand why issues happened in the past, and you can plan for future interactions.[1]

Let's imagine a day when you didn't get a handover. What would your level of stress be? You would have to look at charts, read the notes and talk to patients to gather information. I haven't nursed for many years, and my stress levels are rising just thinking about it. You may experience a drop in status because you feel like you're not being treated with respect. Not getting handover might threaten autonomy due to a lack of choice to use or ignore the information handed over. Relatedness is triggered as you are being ignored. The fairness alarm going off could be the expectation to do your job well even though you haven't had a proper handover, which is unfair. You can see how applicable the SCARF model is.[2]

Maslow's hierarchy of needs says people satisfy their needs in sequence, with physical and safety first. Social and self-esteem needs come next, and then self-actualisation. However, many studies say the brain equates social needs to survival needs, like hunger. We're at work for most of our week. Meeting our social needs is paramount. By now, you can see our social needs are not just social

---

1   Dr David Rock outlines a lot of this research in his book *Your Brain at Work: Strategies for overcoming distraction, regaining focus and working smarter all day long.*

2   If you are interested in your hierarchy of motivation and stress, you can do an online SCARF model assessment through the NeuroLeadership Institute: www.neuroleadership. com/research/tools/nli-scarf-assessment.

activities with others. You can see how a social brain gets triggered in many ways at work, and you, as a leader, can minimise that threat.

To prevent offending someone and to get your team on board, you can use the SCARF model for planning before you want to address an issue at a meeting. For example, you can ensure you're:

- being respectful
- being transparent with the why
- being inclusive
- providing certainty through clear communication.

If possible, provide a choice about actions, even if it's just between two options.

Think about someone you don't get on well with and use the SCARF model to plan your communications with this person. Planning ahead saves you time, and hours sorting out miscommunication. Experiment for yourself and assess if it saves time and improves your confidence in communicating with your team.[3]

CONCLUSION

You have become a leader worth following when you keep your team's needs in mind before you act and speak. You've learned how to keep your team engaged by discovering the drivers of status, certainty, autonomy, relatedness and fairness, as seen in the SCARF model. This same list must be front of mind to prevent potential rifts in relationships and any stress or drama. You've also discovered

---

3   Go to this link to get a useful SCARF handout: c4consultancy.com.au/scarf-worksheet. In this handout, I've listed actions to get the reward response in a team member, and also what actions might trigger the stress response.

the power struggles in all relationships and who you need to be to become a transformational leader. Be more lion – be less cocky, mumma bear, lamb or hyena. By using the lens of dysfunctional and transformational nurse identities, you will not only understand the dynamics around you but you will be able to be who you need to be for your team.

Stop yourself when you're being triggered by another or when you find yourself getting drawn into a bonding pattern. You can start by taking a breath and noticing the dynamics. This is the most empowering thing you can do for yourself and your team. Try it at home. I've been told it has saved and enriched many personal relationships.

Now you know the interactions which create dramas and power struggles in the ward. The next chapter is about adults in charge. We'll tease out the elements of being in adult mode at work. To be more lion. You'll also look at yourself and your team through the lens of personality. Knowing this helps utilise your team's strengths and differences to encourage inclusivity and embrace diversity.

6

Adults in charge

LEADING YOURSELF MUST COME FIRST

You take on higher duties when you step up into a higher role. Higher duties can also call for an improved quality of thinking, coming from a higher level of understanding. The understanding to look for what others need to get the job done, thrive and stay. Your clinical knowledge has made you a great nurse, and coming from this higher level of self will make you a great leader.

Being in the transformational nurse identity of lion – in adult mode – will reduce your stress and improve the type of leader you are for your team. This chapter will focus on how to stay in lion mode at work. This forms the foundation to differentiate further the skills and identity required to be an unleavable leader, which we identify in the next chapter. As a leader, you aspire to higher levels of personal and professional development to stop reactivity.

According to Michael Hyatt, 'How we lead ourselves in life impacts how we lead those around us.' Michael Hyatt is an author, podcaster, blogger and the CEO of Michael Hyatt & Company.

He's written several books about leadership, productivity and goal setting. To raise ourselves above the level of reactivity we must be in the here and now, not triggered by the past. It's taking yourself lightly and others lightly.

Being the lion allows you to accept other personality types and not judge them. Understanding personality types is a way to accept yourself and others. We will use the DISC model in this chapter as a way to appreciate why your team behaves as they do. Acknowledging the why behind any behaviour increases your ability to appreciate, respect and even celebrate their differences.

Dale Carnegie, known for corporate, public speaking and interpersonal skills training, points towards a powerful place to be in life. He says, 'People rarely succeed unless they have fun in what they are doing.' It doesn't mean you have to be laughing and joking all the time – although that would be pretty awesome. It means keeping the high standards with work but being lighter with people. Reduce your intensity and treat people lightly. Being the lion is a low-stress and relational place. It's better for you and your team – there's less drama, better performance, and everybody's mind is on the job.

Muslim Shah, a lecturer and researcher at the Rehman College of Nursing, Pakistan, states that a reduction in conflict occurs when 'interpersonal relationships have cooperation, collaboration, listening and respect the values and position of each other.' You can only have this level of collaboration, listening and respecting another person if you're the lion.

A new nurse leader in coronary care I coached had trouble allocating new patients. When giving instructions to her team, she would yo-yo from super apologetic as the lamb to a very directive cockatoo. If anyone got annoyed, she became defensive and turned into a snappy hyena. But when she learned about adult mode, she communicated differently. She was assertive and would listen, and because she wasn't defensive, she was able to troubleshoot if there was an issue. Most importantly, her confidence soared. She had a new way of talking to her team by embodying the lion.

When you're present, you can have more access to the thinking part of your brain. Being present helps with the self-regulation of emotions and assists with inhibiting thoughts that aren't useful.

In this chapter, you'll learn more about yourself and your team's personality, and why some people get on your nerves when others don't. When people annoy you, it can throw you into the cockatoo (critical parent) mode or the hyena (rebellious teenager) mode. We will explore the notion of being in this non-reactive lion mode at work, which operates in the present, reduces the risk of reactive relationships and increases the likelihood of being an unleavable leader.

BE THE LION

Change in your leadership behaviour can only happen when you shift your identity. The lion is open, rational and nonjudgmental, but what does being the lion feel like? You feel confident but not overconfident or cocky (ha-ha, I love using these animals!). You're open to ideas but also value your own. You trust your abilities because you understand your strengths but are available to look at others' strengths. It feels even and balanced.

To help you lead as the lion, you must understand the principles of being an unleavable leader. Eric Berne, the psychoanalyst who founded Transactional Analysis, says there are a few philosophies you need to consider when you're coming from this place inside you:

- People are essentially good – 'I'm okay, and you are okay.'
- Every human can think and learn. It's a promotion of self-determination and action coming from self-determination.
- Being aware of the unconscious patterns gives you the ability to shift from one to another when needed.

What's in it for you?

In chapter 5, we explored nurse identities in relation to others and divided them into dysfunctional and transformational identities. You can also use these parts in how you relate to yourself. It is still a relationship model, but this time it reveals how you relate to two aspects: your thoughts and your feelings, and situations in your life.

For example, having the cockatoo in your head means you are going to be critical of your thoughts, and you're going to have high standards for yourself. When you have high standards for yourself, you've got high standards with others and have many 'shoulds'.

Coming from the lamb means you are looking at problems rather than solutions. You're thinking, *poor me. I'm not good enough.* You're a victim of every thought that comes into your head.

Coming from mumma bear means you're going to rescue yourself. You're going to avoid challenging situations. You rescue yourself by saying no to challenges and opportunities. You'll save yourself from feelings using alcohol or even binge-watching Netflix.

But when you are the lion with yourself, you put situations and thoughts into perspective. You shift from 'should' to 'could'. You look at what you can and can't control and can laugh at yourself. You're objective and rational and feel emotions but are not overrun by them. You can label these parts and point to them. Doing this turns off your stress response, which allows the higher order thinking required to lead yourself and others and have a great life.

To get into lion mode, you can use cognitive reappraisal – meaning you reinterpret and reframe things because it's useful. An example of cognitive reappraisal might be if you're starting to compare yourself to other people, or put others on a pedestal. A reframe would be, *I have different strengths and I do things differently*, or, *I'm seeing one aspect of this, not another*. In this mode, you won't be influenced so easily by others.

The Milgram obedience study by Stanley Milgram from Yale University changed how we view obedience to authority figures. The results were shocking. Men aged 20 to 50, of varying occupations and levels of education, were encouraged by an experimenter in a white coat to shock other people with electricity. The participants were told they were helping discover how people learn. They were told the shock levels were at what's considered painful and potentially lethal levels. But unbeknown to the participants, it was all fake. A high proportion obeyed the instructions, even though they could hear the person (an actor) scream in apparent reaction to the supposed shocks. The researchers surmised that compliance occurred because a person in a white coat gave the instructions. And it was a formal setting, and they were getting paid to do it.

Does this sound similar to a hospital to you?

Obedience is ingrained in us from childhood. Awareness is needed to navigate this culturally ingrained system to be a transformational leader and transform healthcare. You need this adult part that can use logic to decide how to act. Being in adult mode feels like you're yourself. It's important to know what adult mode feels like because it can be a considerable risk to be reactive and sit as a leader in a dysfunctional nurse identity like the cockatoo or blindly follow like a lamb.

Try noticing when you do feel even and objective. Is it on your days off, or do you feel like this at work? You can only be the lion when you come from the principle *I'm okay, you are okay*, and feel people are equal to you. Think of when you were in a relationship that worked – perhaps a friendship or with a sibling or a partner. How did they treat you, and how did you treat them? How did it make you feel? Could you have been in adult mode then? Did you listen? Did you go for a win–win if there was a conflict? Did you get a sense you accepted them the way they were, and they accepted you the way you were? Or did it feel like you were playing a game of one-upmanship, riding your high horse of righteousness or walking on eggshells?

You may often come from the lion in your relationship with your partner. But sometimes, you may shift into these dysfunctional identities that create drama and reactivity. Again, this is normal – we're human and get triggered by each other.

Remember when I told you the story about Camelot in chapter 4? Being in adult mode is like Camelot. Instead of a long table with somebody at the head holding the power, it's a round table where all are equal.

Getting into adult mode is difficult when you're stressed and emotional. James Gross, a professor of psychology at Stanford, said emotions are brief responses that affect the body's physiology and behaviour. Emotions are important as they are generated in situations that may be a challenge or an opportunity. Gross, an expert in emotional regulation, says there are three ways to reduce emotions:

- **Expressing them:** for example, by crying. Not the best option at work, but sharing with someone you trust is good.

- **Expressive suppression:** trying to stop the emotion being perceived by others. This seems strange to the observer. They can sense you're pushing down a feeling. Gross found this increases the inner stress response and your blood pressure. It takes up a lot of brain power, and performance goes down, as does memory and focus.
- **Cognitive change:** reappraising what the situation means to you. This is the best solution. When nurse leaders feel under enormous pressure, they can shift their focus to experience the hustle and bustle and even enjoy watching the dance of it all fitting together in an imperfect way. Change your story, which changes your focus, which changes your energy and responses to your team.

Being in lion mode means that you are present, non-judgemental and not stressed. Thinking kind thoughts about others generates kind feelings and the hormone oxytocin. Oxytocin allows you to feel love, care and trust. Dr David Hamilton in his book *The Five Side Effects of Kindness* says that kindness is contagious and it operates as the opposite of stress. He explains that peace and calm is not the opposite of stress, merely the absence of it. Kindness and stress are opposites and if one goes up the other goes down. Thinking kind thoughts keeps you in adult mode and makes it more likely your team member will respond in adult mode back. And with kindness as it is contagious.

Overcoming dysfunctional nurse identities and cognitive distortions

Using the principles of transformational nurse identities listed earlier in this chapter can help with a cognitive change. The shift that is often required is one of perspective – a perspective shift of the situation, yourself or the person you are interacting with. Aaron Beck is a psychiatrist and is regarded as the father of cognitive behaviour therapy. Many people know it as CBT. He named the ways of thinking that negatively skew how we see the world, ourselves and others 'cognitive distortions'.

As the cockatoo (critical parent) or mumma bear (nurturing parent/rescuer), you would be overgeneralising, which is the cognitive distortion of believing that future events will be the same as past events – such as, *all junior nurses are the same* (personalisation as well). In this mode you would minimise some positive aspects of a person or their strengths and maximise problems or catastrophise, expecting the worst. This leads to pressure and you taking on too much responsibility. You might think in black and white, with no middle ground. This cognitive distortion makes you use the words 'should', 'always' and 'never'. Another cocky and mumma bear cognitive distortion could be labelling – and mis-labelling – people and situations. 'He is a whiner', or, 'she is hopeless' are examples, and overgeneralisation will soon move in to create more stress and excessive responsibility on your side and blame on the other.

The lamb (adapted child/victim) would use the cognitive distortion of personalisation – blaming themselves for things they have no control over, such as the actions of others. The lamb can also create stress by jumping to conclusions, catastrophising and 'mind reading'. Mind reading is when you think you know what other people are thinking. Emotional reasoning is another distortion that keeps you in the lamb, which also causes stress. You jump to a conclusion and ignore facts as you listen to your feelings first. In emotional reasoning, you feel tired and overwhelmed, so your mind reasons the situation must be beyond what you can solve.

When you are more lion, you can make the cognitive shift from these dysfunctional nurse identities and see the cognitive distortions for what they are. Becoming objective, you simply notice and name the cognitive distortions as you learn that's what your mind is doing.

A reappraisal is changing the interpretation of an event. For example, shifting from, *this is a disaster*, to, *this is bad but manageable*. Then your mind shifts focus from the problem to breaking it down into possible solutions. A shift in focus is powerful – from *these people are out to get me*, to *this is not personal; they are doing the best they can, just like me*. These ideas help you with stress as it comes up in the moment on shift. Mindful naming is also useful; for example, *I'm noticing I'm feeling a bit anxious.*

There are many other actions you can take to assist you with stress. You change the emotional state by using the box breathing (chapter 3) or any deep breathing. The Emotional Freedom Technique (EFT), or 'tapping' as it is known, can turn off the stress response. I have found this technique useful. I refer my clients to Brad Yates, an expert in EFT who has over 600 videos on YouTube. Search for his name and what you want help with: stress, anxiety, sleep or confidence. You will get strange looks while tapping in public. It is perfect to use in the bathroom at work or in the privacy of your home.

UNDERSTANDING AND ACCEPTING ALL PERSONALITIES

An essential aspect of adult mode is being able to appreciate yourself and see yourself clearly, as well as appreciating others' strengths even though they're different. It's important to view yourself and others with an attitude of kindness and compassion.

The DISC model

To help you understand your personality we will look at the DISC model, first described by psychologist Dr William Marston in 1928. In his book *The Emotions of Normal People*, he theorised people are motivated to act by four intrinsic drives or tendencies: dominance, influence, steadiness and compliance. These tendencies have a combination of reservation, outgoingness, and being more task-oriented or people-oriented.

Some nurses I've spoken to admit to being more task- than relationship-focused. If this is you, you can cultivate both brain networks. Research by neuroscientist and psychologist Anthony Jack showed we can switch from being one to another. Jack found the brain has task-positive networks, which are analytical and task-oriented, and a default mode network which is empathetic and social. It takes some energy to switch from one to the other, but it can be done. Both task and relationship strengths are required to be a good nurse leader. This book seeks to help all nurse leaders give directions in a way that keeps relationships healthy.

The DISC model has a four-quadrant framework:

- **Dominance** is how we respond to problems and challenges.
- **Influence** is how we respond to people.
- **Steadiness** is how we react to pace and consistency at work.
- **Compliance** is how we respond to procedures and complaints.

It's great to know there's no right or wrong with personality – each person has a preference, and each style has its strengths and weaknesses. Once you understand each personality type has strengths and limitations, you'll judge yourself and others less.[1] When I learned about my partner's personality type, I swear it saved our relationship because I shifted from judging to thinking, *that's why he does this!* He's so detail-oriented, and I'm not. I'm big-picture thinking (and I forget to shut cupboards). I began to appreciate his strengths and therefore appreciate him more.

It's helpful if you and your leadership team come to understand your individual communication styles. This allows appreciation of the potential communication strengths of each person and shows you how to adjust to cater for their style. For instance, if you are more direct and like to get to the point straight away (directive), you may have to first soften your approach to someone who likes small talk.

You might think *I don't like being labelled*, but this is just one way to understand your and other people's behaviours and communication styles. It points towards something, but it's not defining you. It's a tool towards understand somebody, like when you take one blood sample. It doesn't explain the whole person. It gives some data on one aspect.

Some have found a free version of this assessment useful when they don't have the budget for the complete version. A free version simplifies the model – for a comprehensive report, you must get a paid version.[2] It is not the only assessment tool for leadership styles, and you may find other ones are as useful. Whatever assessment you do, don't limit viewing the report to understanding *your* style. Understand and appreciate others' styles as well. It will help

---

1 Here is a link to a free and elementary version of the DISC assessment: www.123test.com/disc-personality-test

2 I'm skilled at giving feedback individually and to groups, so you can contact me if you would like a consultant who can help with DISC assessments in the healthcare sector. I can show you how these personality traits play out on the floor.

you gain a holistic view of the personalities within your team and plan your communication. In my leadership masterminds, we use the DISC report as a personal plan for development.

Being able to interpret the communication needs of others can make you a master communicator. If you want to improve your communication with those who are not in your style, you'll be more effective if you follow these tips:

- You need to stick to the point when talking to **dominant** people. You don't need to build rapport with these people. You need to be organised, clear and brief because they want to get to the bottom line and move forward.
- For those high in **influence**, you need to be warm and friendly. You need to give lots of words of appreciation. Feel free to talk about your feelings with them. If you are sharing detailed information, give it to them in written form rather than talking too much about it because they'll get lost.
- You need to ease into the conversation with rapport building for those high in **steadiness**. These folk want you to take a slower approach. Don't rush them to speak. Ask questions and give them space to answer.
- **Compliance** folk are those who love systems and are detail orientated. Make sure you stay on task by giving them accurate information and processes. Don't rush them as they want to answer in the right way. They love to 'measure four times and cut once', so be prepared, organised and patient with them.

The first step is to have an awareness of your style and preference. Note which of the communication styles listed above seem more natural for you. You may feel resonance with two of these.

These descriptions might remind you of someone you know. If that's the case, practise with them and watch how your interactions improve. You may have to practise varying your communication style as it will not come easy.

Differences are required

High-performing clinical teams need all personality types, and one of the principles of a transformational leader is to appreciate everyone. Think of the human body. We have many different looking and functioning organs. They are all essential to the body's running, and (usually) work together beautifully. Their differences are appreciated and required. Understanding the differences in personality in your team can reduce blame and cognitive biases while improving relationships. As the lion, you will accept without judgement, but that's not always easy. Whenever you think of someone, you are cognitively appraising them. Kevin Ochsner at Columbia University studies the neuroscience of appraisal building. He explains that our emotional responses flow from how we think of others and a situation. Change the thought, change the emotion. He said, 'If our emotional responses fundamentally flow out of interpretations or appraisal of the world and we can change those appraisals, then we have to try and do so. And not to do so at some level is rather irresponsible.' To lead well is to not get sloppy with your thinking and reactions so you can lead those different from you.

The differences could be race, skin colour, personality, age, gender or even football team. Have you ever wondered why defence lawyers want jurors who view the defendant as similar to them? In an article on the website Science and the Big Questions named 'Why Your Brain Hates Other People and How to Make it Think Differently', Robert Sapolsky wrote that we forgive people who are in our 'in' group or similar to us for their transgressions. Defence lawyers want a jury who thinks the defendant is in their 'in' group. To operate out of your transformational nurse identity as a leader, you need to understand inclusivity and accept you have a natural bias against other people who are different. Human resources, or people and culture as this group is often called today, encourages diversity and talks about inclusivity. With more international nurses used for shortages in our hospital system and primary care teams, nurse leaders need to be able to understand diversity and inclusion. When you learn about people's personalities and understand the biases we all have, you revolutionalise your leadership, accepting of other people and who acknowledges them.

Sapolsky says when others look different 'there is a preferential activation of the amygdala'. As we stated in the previous chapter, the amygdala is the alarm system in the brain that turns on the stress response. The notion of 'us' and 'them' is hardwired in our system, says Sapolsky. You will recollect from chapter 2 Kahneman calls this system one thinking. It's emotional, and it's automatic. Sapolsky tells the story of the filming of the 1968 version of *Planet of the Apes* where, at lunchtime, those playing the monkeys and those playing the gorillas ate in separate groups. According to Sapolsky, there are two kinds of people: those who divide and those who don't. He states that more people divide everyone into 'us' and 'them' than don't. Which one are you? But more importantly, which one will you *choose* to be?

Cliques or 'in groups' do have their place. Initially, when someone joins a group, you get a sense of belonging – as you join a warm fuzzy 'us'. When the 'us versus them' mentality begins, you communicate differently from your in-group to the out-group. If you aren't aware of this intrinsic bias, it becomes dangerous.

Your teams will get stressed due to a lack of fairness. Don't be lured into thinking they can't feel it. They can.

For clarity on how different personalities are practical at work, list the different roles in the unit. Think about which personality style might do best with particular tasks. For example, an auditor is an excellent job for those who love systems and compliance, while the social committee might be better for those with high scores in influence who enjoy connecting with people. There's a job for everyone in the unit. Another thing you can do is have more contact with those in another group. Share stories to discover similarities. Once you understand similarities between you, you can shift them in your mind from the 'out' group to your 'in' group.

Remember that emotions are like a genie if you are dealing with somebody you don't like. Don't let them out of the bottle. Don't let your feelings get traction. It'll be like a snowball running down a hill.

You may not think you have biases. Try not to see biases as good or bad. See them for what they are. It's an energy-saving part of being human that has its place. But the place is not at work. Shift to system two thinking and root out those pesky biases.

CONCLUSION

You have taken some significant steps towards being the adult in the room of reactivity. This knowledge can allow you to stand out as a leader and lead the revolution to lead better in nursing. Personality assessments always interest people, as we love to understand ourselves more. You've discovered all strengths are welcome in the ward. You've also got a fresh way of looking at others to appreciate their strengths. Especially with the recruitment of more international nurses, we need to understand implicit biases and rise above them.

Stop assuming your first response is always the proper response. Just because it feels comfortable doesn't mean it's right. It's time to discontinue acceptance of reactivity and drama as the norm. Let's start with a new vision of what healthcare and nursing can be. Imagine a whole world filled with people acting like adults. Accept this call to higher duties – not doing more, but being more adult, more objective, more self-aware and less reactive – more lion.

In chapter 7, we tease apart the lion (adult mode) into four new transformational nurse identities. You will learn how to get from the dysfunctional nurse identities – cockatoo, mumma bear, hyena and lamb – to ones that get tasks done, that will also engage your team and help them learn.

7

The catalyst, the creator, the challenger and the coach

TRANSFORMING YOURSELF

To his surprise, on 1 April 1953, Dag Hammarskjold, a 49-year-old Swedish delegate to the United Nations, was elected Secretary-General. When advised of this by a reporter, he thought it was an April fool's day joke. Dag Hammarskjold was humble, and the youngest person to hold this prestigious and influential position. He epitomised Transformational Leadership as he walked around every UN department to shake hands. Dag ate in the main cafeteria as much as possible. He gave over his private elevator to general use. While using his time in the role to facilitate peace, he also had to make hard decisions, like where to place peacekeeping forces and where not to. He created a space all people could visit to get quiet during the day. He advocated for personal development. He said: 'While many believe that transforming organisations ... is the most difficult, the truth is that transforming ourselves is the hardest job. If we transform ourselves, we transform the world.' Your team requires you to continue to evolve. Your vision for your unit and healthcare needs you to continue this journey. This chapter presents a shift into the four selves of being a present, deliberate, transformational leader.

Let's start with a recap. Chapter 5 taught you about the three modes: parent, adult and child. You discovered that as a leader, you can trigger your team to respond in a way that distracts them from working well, increases the drama and reduces engagement and retention. In chapter 6, I converted these parts that trigger and transform others into nursing identities: dysfunctional and trans-formational. In my lighthearted way, I made them more accessible to you by making them animals!

In chapter 6, you learned how to operate in an adult mode that engages your team and allows them to feel respected and like an equal, a true partner in healthcare. In this chapter, I have combined the building blocks from Transformational Leadership outlined in chapter 1 with the lion (adult) parts of you. These parts will enable you to lead the revolution healthcare needs when you activate them.

Transforming yourself is the shift from the unconsciously triggered nurse identities to their countertypes. The countertype transformational nursing identities are the way out of being a leader your team wants to leave. They are the escape route from being stuck in the cockatoo, mumma bear, lamb or hyena. The transformational nurse identities are:

- the catalyst
- the creator
- the challenger
- the coach.

They also each have an animal identity, and you will meet them in this chapter. It is intentional that three of the four animals I have chosen are mammals that take care of their young.

I was inspired to create and map these parts to help make nursing leadership easier by utilising the work of Acey Choy. Choy's *Winner's Triangle* was his contribution to remedying the 'stuckness' individuals experience in the Drama Triangle. I wasn't just inspired to create these transformational nurse identities; I was asked. Many of my clients requested training to stay in lion more, with a sustainable way to think about getting out of the dysfunctional parts.

There is an overlap between Choy's winner's triangle and the model of Transformational Leadership described in chapter 1. I have named this combined model of the winner's triangle and Transformational Leadership the Transformational Nurse Identities (TNI) model. Using this model results in empowerment out of drama and reactivity. These parts or transformational nurse identities – just like the cockatoo (critical parent), mumma bear (nurturing parent/rescuer), lion (adult), lamb (adapted child/victim) and hyena (rebellious teenager) – have thoughts, feelings, beliefs systems and a particular way of acting.

You can develop these parts or identities (I will still use these words interchangeably) upon learning their functions, practising their skills, noticing when you have used them in the past, and through self-reflection. After learning about these identities in this chapter, you will hone them further in chapter 9. Shifting between parts means holding the parts of yourself lightly and being flexible. It's about being adaptive, which is another way of describing psychological flexibility.

Psychological flexibility is acting on values and goals rather than impulses. To manage this, you must be objective with your thoughts, feelings and goals, and when you respond to others in your environment. It's mindfulness again! Or the aspect of mindfulness when you acknowledge you are not your thoughts but the thinker of them. You don't let them own you. Be in lion with them, not the lamb! Or the cocky, getting critical with them and others.

Psychological flexibility is learnable.[1] Responding to the environment means shifting to the part that's right for the context. Treating an event with seriousness yet holding it lightly to be flexible is possible. When you are psychologically flexible, you are not fixed on one solution being the only way; you are less anxious and more able to see all sides. For perfectionists, you will find this a relief because there is a letting go of being right. Edward de Bono, said to be the master of how to think, claims a discussion should be a genuine attempt to explore a subject lightly rather than a battle between competing egos. He says, 'Holding something lightly would be how to have a beautiful mind'. A beautiful mind leads the way to a beautiful relationship with your team. A beautiful mind exists in a composed brain. A composed brain can sit with the uncertainty of these times and lead out of healthcare's mess.

And do you know what else? Your leadership journey creates a happier you. You can't not be happier when you develop and evolve your relationships and your mind in this way.

Finding an easy way out of the work dramas into transformational leadership and relationships will make you a leader for the times. In the complex, high-pressure workplaces of today, you need to be adaptable and shifting from one part to another part.

This chapter reveals who you need to be and how to get there. The reactive nurse identities of the cocky, lamb, hyena and

---

1   According to Todd Kashdan and Jonathan Rottenberg in their 2002 Clinical Psychological Review article, 'Psychological Flexibility as a Fundamental Aspect of Health'.

mumma bear feel sticky and hard to escape. When we're in the stress response, these parts are persuasive, and it feels as if you must continue to think, feel and act the same way. Another path is becoming the counterparts for the dysfunctional parts: the catalyst, the creator, the challenger and the coach. The Transformational Nurse Identities.

THE WISDOM AND UTILITY OF PRESENCE

It's easier to get in touch with these transformational nurse identities when you're ready to be deliberate, present and composed. Each dysfunctional nurse identity has a countertype that will make you unleavable. Nurse leaders have told me it's comforting to know there is a way out. With a focus shift, you can act, think and feel differently. The added benefit of being present is that it reduces your stress response.

Being present means you can lead from who you are now, not who you were in the past. You'll be less reactive. Learning how to do it in the moment means it's practical. Kristen Hansen, a leadership speaker and expert on the brain, stated that taking brain breaks allows the prefrontal cortex – the thinking part of your brain – to quieten. This means you create the conditions required to receive an insight or an a-ha moment and open yourself to get out of a rut of thinking.

Staying composed requires identifying emotions and emotional states. David Creswell, a neuroscientist at UCLA, studies emotional regulation and found that those who are mindful and name their emotions turn off their amygdala – the alarm switch in the brain. An example being, there's the feeling of anxiety. When you're objective and unreactive, you can name how you feel. Doing this can shift you to a more effective nurse identity.

You might say, 'It's hard to be mindful at work. There's so much going on.' When approached at work in a drama state, sometimes you need some phrases to buy yourself some time to get more objective. Mindfulness is getting into an objective mind; then it is easy to pivot from the reactive way of responding to a countertype that is more useful for the moment. To buy some time, say, 'Okay, that's good to know. Can I get back to you?' You can think about where you need to redirect focus. Do you need to reframe the statement for them? Perhaps they need to know what to focus on next, and you can coach them into finding their answers.

Use 'veto power' to cut out mental noise. Veto power is where you choose what you think using focus and deciding what thoughts to shut out. You do this already. An easy example is the idea of thinking about sex at work. If you did, you would use veto power to shut that down, as it isn't useful. You can veto certain thoughts when it's not the right time. It can give your mind space to think about important issues.

It may seem like a long shot for your mind to accept this, but spiritual teacher and author of *The Power of Now* Eckart Tolle says:

> *All problems are illusions of the mind. Focus your attention on the now and tell me what problem you have at this moment. I am not getting any answer because it is impossible to have a problem when your attention is fully in the Now. A situation needs to be either dealt with or accepted. Why make it into a problem?*

How good would that be? No problems! I need to admit that this is a work in progress for me. But when I get it, I get it, and my perception of a situation changes dramatically.

You don't have to be present all the time. *Thinking about* being present isn't unusual. You can switch from being present to thinking and then back again. You already do it, but we're talking about doing it deliberately, meaning you're not lost in thoughts and labelling things as a problem – you can take a step back and be objective.

Nurses I work with sometimes grow frustrated with the idea of mindfulness when their working day feels so busy. But Eckhart Tolle says mindfulness can be practical. A peaceful, flexible mind is possible with mini meditations. These enable you to step out of your standard train of thought. It can take one to fifteen seconds to build awareness of your breath and anchor your mind there. Allow yourself to notice the breath entering your nose, and its path as it travels down into your lungs, expanding your chest and abdomen. Tolle says, ' ... notice what it feels like in your body to be alive'. Another way is by noticing your thoughts and feelings as they arise, like passing cars. Or clouds floating by. Say to yourself: *there's a feeling, that's a thought.*

> Reflect on:
>
> **Self-awareness:** How can you use this when you're walking around the ward? I would pretend I was walking around in a video game, giving myself an avatar. When you do this, you sense the space around you. You notice your arms and legs as they're moving, and you notice your thoughts as they arise. Ask yourself, *Is the person in this video game getting caught up in their thinking? What will be the outcome if they do? Can they focus on the next challenge as it arises in the video game? Or are they caught up in their thoughts?*

My clients also find it useful when walking to slow their pace for a few moments. To momentarily tune into their body moving, arms swinging. Or use their breath as an anchor. When stressed sometimes, it's easier to listen to the ward sounds.

Don't be fooled by these seemingly simple strategies. Shifting your mind like this makes your thinking system shift, making you more efficient, even and objective. It's normal to think you can't do it, and it's a failure because your mind keeps interrupting you. If you're like many, you know meditation can be essential, but your mind tells you that you don't have enough time to take 15 seconds to focus. But you do. It's a high-leverage activity that will make your work life easier. As the saying goes, 'If you don't have time to meditate for an hour every day, you should meditate for two hours.'

Think it's silly to talk about this in a leadership book? Being present is accepting all arising thoughts, even the ones that say it's silly. Being mindful allows them to come and go without fighting them, and just attending to useful thoughts. Once you know what your thoughts say to you, my bet is you will be surprised. Many can be pretty ridiculous. Rather than your thoughts dragging you around, see them for what they are: mostly random. You don't need to listen to them all.

Many people find mindfulness boring, but I invite you to think of it differently. Those who ride motorbikes know the feeling of being mindful when riding. They have to be present to stay alive, and aware of their surroundings. They feel like they're in their body riding rather than their mind drifting. It's a matter of survival, but they also report feeling most alive when riding. They love it. Maybe you can think like that at work.

For my honours thesis, I used an experimental design to look at the impact of positive emotions on mindfulness and cognitive flexibility. I discovered that those who were more positive had higher scores for mindfulness. Increasing your positivity means you will be more psychologically flexible and adaptive. If you feel optimistic about what is happening, you are less caught up in thinking about the past or the future. You are also less critical.

Use gratitude. Gratitude aligns your focus to what is going well, which reduces the stress response and increases positivity – and, therefore, the likelihood of presence. You could also try dancing, laughing and shaking your body. Small things will change your focus and your physiology. Every thought, action and feeling changes the chemistry in your body, moment to moment.

THE COUNTERTYPE TRANSFORMATIONAL NURSING IDENTITIES

The countertype transformational nursing identities are the escape route from the cockatoo, mumma bear, lamb or hyena. (I hope the animals help you modify your leadership, keeping it light and fresh.)

Eagle the catalyst

Unlike the other three transformational nurse identities in this chapter, the catalyst did not arise from a countertype from a dysfunctional nurse identity. This leadership identity is drawn from the building block of Transformational Leadership. Self-deliberate leadership is the goal of the catalyst, which creates the vision and is a role model for energy, optimism and professionalism. The natural creature for the catalyst is the eagle. The eagle is fearless as it swoops from massive heights to catch its prey, showing tenacity and great vision. Eagles see a long way ahead, which is perfect for a visionary. And eagles communicate in many different ways, including complex flying routines, special movements and different sounds.

The three keywords for eagle are catalyser, visionary and communicator:

- Catalyser:
    - manages their energy and their team's
    - optimistic and looks to the future
    - strategises and enables focus on the right goals
    - provides a role model of clinical knowledge and professional attitude.

- Visionary:
    - asks, 'how can we do this?'
    - knows their why
    - connects to a meaning and purpose
    - is a big-picture thinker – sees the hospital as a system and themselves as a part of the wider community and world.

- Communicator:
    - communicates through different mediums to keep the team up to date
    - knows how to use stories to motivate and share a vision
    - knows their team's motivations and communicates the team's motivators, not their own.

Inspiring your team allows them to connect to something higher. The motivation to work becomes intrinsic rather than needing an extrinsic motivator, like more pay. As a leader, you're saying, 'come – follow me'. Why would they follow you unless you had a vision or inspired them to work independently? If you don't have a dream, you're more a manager than a leader.

Transformational leadership aspects of the catalyst (eagle)

Transformational Leadership's building block for the catalyst is 'inspirational motivation'. In this aspect, the nurse leader creates a vision and communicates it in a way the team can see and follow. This nurse mode shares a vision energetically, sets inspiring goals, has high expectations, is optimistic and connects to a sense of meaning.

The feedback I received from a nurse leader after a visioning workshop was that working with her vision and purpose meant that the little things at work didn't bother her. They seemed small in comparison. The vision gave her perspective.

The trend I've noticed in nursing is that nurses need to be more adaptive, move to other wards, and be flexible when required. A nursing director in a large city hospital was trialling a way to share experience and resources between two critical care wards. She gave them autonomy around organising this and shared with them compelling reasons. The two nurse unit managers were excited about the changes and participated eagerly with rolling it out. However, the nurse unit managers communicated the roll out from their level: flexibility, career progression, and patient outcomes. The nurse leaders could agree on how it should unfold, but on each shift it was clunky, and out of hours the nurses in charge would argue, each fighting for their patch. They felt it affected their status to help next door and give up resources (like ECG machines and temporary pacemakers), and they wanted certainty about when they were getting them back. They also didn't comprehend why it was important for them. There was no trust between the teams, relatedness or motivation. Remember how important these are in the SCARF model. What would you do if you were the director of these critical care areas? What would you have done to get these nurses on board?

Many practical nurses find the idea of a vision hard to grasp. They tend to work shift to shift and think of solutions for problems, not imagine a vision. If this is you, take heart. Think of possibilities. Take a risk and ask, what if? What have you always wanted to change? Mark Johnson and Josh Suskewicz, authors of *Lead from the Future: How to turn visionary thinking into breakthrough growth*, state, 'Strategy is a way to win a game. Vision tells you what game to play.'

As a leader, you need to know what game you're playing. You already have a vision; we all do. It just might not be a good one. If you talk negatively about work, that is your vision. It's not an inspiring one. What is that automatic image you have of work? What would happen if you found one more inspiring and started working from that? How would working from a positive vision change the way you lead, and how would you describe it to your team? What sort of energy would you bring to work each day if you had an inspiring vision?

The eagle is the inner fire that gets me out of bed and moving. Eagle reminds me of what is important in each moment, connects me to my values and vision of what's possible, and feeds my optimism for the future. I would not spend countless hours writing this book if I didn't have a vision of how I could help leaders like yourself feel more hopeful about your leadership. This will help the nurses you lead want to come to work.

Reflect on:

Social regulation: Think about when you were excited about something and convinced others about the idea. It could be your children, your partner or your friends. You could have persuaded them to take a particular holiday or go to an event or to eat their broccoli. How did you do this? Did you paint a picture of the result? Or did you threaten them or punish them? What were your energy levels like when you were talking about what was important to you?

If you believe in a future visionary state in your unit, you need to know what it is and supply the fuel to get you there. Attend seminars that inspire you, read books about leaders who do inspiring things, and watch some TED Talks.

★ **Be more eagle:** be courageous enough to light the way with vision and strategy.

Dolphin the creator

Lamb (adapted child/victim) is when you feel like a victim, feel less than others and get stuck focusing on the problem and what you can't do. The lamb is a very stressful and heavy dysfunctional nurse identity to be stuck in. The creator is the countertype to the lamb. The animal that fits is the dolphin. The dolphin is said to have self-awareness and be one of the smartest animals. It is a lighter, smarter, more playful part of you. This part loves to experiment, has compassion for themselves and others, and uses their smarts when it reduces stress by solving problems. I like to think that the dolphin is a solution-seeking mammal. There are three main aspects to dolphin the creator:

- Experimental:
  - can try something new – says 'let's experiment'
  - tries to look at situations from another perspective.
- Compassionate:
  - admits to humanity and vulnerability
  - says 'it's normal sometimes to get lost and feel helpless'
  - knows you're not alone – 'we are a team'
  - owns their feelings, thoughts and vulnerability
  - knows it's okay to ask for help.

- Solution-seeking:
  - 'this is a feeling, and I could be catastrophising'
  - notices this in self and others
  - reduces stress by focusing on solving problems and looking for solutions.

You can shift to this part when you're feeling defeated. You can get the brain back into the reward state with the dolphin's cognitive and creative capacity. To shift from lamb to dolphin can feel like a significant change – from a state of feeling helpless and defeated to focused on goals and optimism. It's powerful.

Transformational leadership aspects of the dolphin

Dolphin is the identity we align with the Transformational Leadership aspect of 'idealised influence'. This building block of Transformational Leadership is humble and intent on getting results through personal responsibility and persistence. People in this mode are said to be charismatic as they listen to team members and focus on the moment. They are a role model of clinical practice, professionalism and respect. They inspire high standards, and staff trust these people. Curiosity, rather than intelligence, is how these leaders succeed.

You might think, *we can't afford to experiment in nursing. We use evidence-based practice.* Every place I've worked seems to do things differently. Even if you haven't moved around, you would have heard nurses say, 'We like to do this at the Alfred.' There is often room to experiment and try new things while keeping evidence-based practices and standards of care. Curiosity is important for listening to new ideas and including your team in continuous improvement.

Sharing and being vulnerable can feel challenging. You must balance over-sharing and keeping some of your feelings to yourself. At the right time, share a vulnerability to increase your relatability with your team. Remember David Rock's SCARF model in chapter 5? Relatability will trigger the rewards response in your team members, making them feel more connected to you and like you're in the 'in' group.

Some of the elements of the dolphin are not always relevant, just as any part of you isn't relevant all the time. Take the experimental aspect. Sometimes you need to go with the tried-and-true methods. It's not always helpful to be solutions-focused when listening to your team members' intense emotions. In psychology, we call this sitting in the mud with them. Let them talk until you feel a shift. The dolphin needs to be selected when it's time for solutions. It is okay to shift into solution-seeking when the action time is time sensitive.

Notice if the lamb is 'running the show' in you. Feeling stuck, pessimistic and unsure is a sure sign the lamb is around, and you need to shift to dolphin the creator. Dolphin has a can-do type of feeling. Do one small task to get some momentum, even if it's making a cup of tea, making a call or putting something away. Remember a time you felt stuck and then found a solution? That's the shift from lamb to dolphin. Lambs can make excuses using obstacles around them. Use the statement, 'given that … '. It means you have considered *that*, but you can move forward anyway. Isn't there always a 'given that' anyway?! Accept it and move out of lamb. Take your power away from the problem and focus on what can be done despite the issues. Take a walk in nature or take a break to get a different perspective. You can shift your attention from what you feel stuck about to something you can do to get a quick win.

Ask for help if required. Break the issue down into small parts. List what you can and can't control, and journal as Rachael Robertson – Antarctica's second woman expedition leader – did.

In dolphin you use reframing. You can ask yourself and your team, *how else can I look at this? What is the positive in this? What can I learn from this? How can I put this into perspective?* These are all excellent questions. How does it feel to be action-oriented and solution-seeking but also kind and patient with others? These are the feelings of dolphin the creator.

When stuck in lamb, it can be easy to listen to the stories in your head that say it won't work. Or your mind can give you excuses: *we've tried it before*, or, *it's not the right time*. It's normal and natural to have those thoughts and observations. What would your inner dolphin say? What vision can you try as an experiment? Who can you get to help? Can you break it down into small parts? Are you focusing on the solution or the problem?

When you're feeling stuck, the thought that 'nothing can help' can be so alluring that you can get more stuck! Get objective and grab a friend. Write in a journal, start doing some goal setting and break down some goals into small actions. Suffering is an option – a change in identity is only a breath away.

★ **Be more dolphin:** think about possibilities, and be open to the size of the solution not needing to equal the size of the problem.

Bonobo the challenger

The cockatoo (critical parent) is the dysfunctional nurse identity who thinks they have more knowledge and power than the team and tries to win rather than negotiate when in conflict. Cocky is around a lot when you are stressed. This part doesn't listen and thinks they're always right. The counterpart for the critical parent is the challenger, and bonobo is the challenger's animal name. A bonobo is a type of chimpanzee, said to be the smartest monkey in the world and most like man. Unlike other primates, they don't have a strict social hierarchy. Scientists joke that the bonobo is 99.4% human. Bonobo speaks frankly, understands others and can set boundaries and standards with compassion. The three keywords to remember with bonobo are frankness, collaboration and flexibility.

- Frank:
  - sets standards and directness with compassion
  - shares knowledge respectfully
  - speaks but notices the other person's reaction
  - states needs with respect
  - able to make hard decisions if required
  - assertive.

- Collaborative:
  - encouraging
  - looking for others' strengths
  - trusts things will happen
  - understands others' needs
  - listens as well as directs – a balance between the two
  - notices that others do well with support.

- Flexible:
  - playful
  - holds self lightly
  - lets go of ego
  - has a softness in demeanour
  - open to other ways of doing the task when required.

Being more bonobo means you are giving directions and taking charge when it's needed. Nurses need a leader who organises well and gives clear, drama-free communication to all the team, not just the nursing team. You will be respected for directing clearly when it counts.

It's easy to see how bonobo is the countertype for the cocky, and leading from this part will help make you a transformational leader. The command-and-control type of leadership of the cocky can wreck relationships, and relationships are how you get things done in the ward. Transforming relationships is also how you increase retention.

Transformational leadership aspects of the bonobo

In the Transformational Leadership model, the building block that is converted to bonobo the challenger is called 'intellectual stimulation'. In intellectual stimulation, the nurse interacts with the team, invites solutions and encourages continuous improvement to grow in their unit. Again, they listen and are open to learning, but they're good at critical thinking, asking questions, curious, and looking at others as willing co-creators. You're doing this part already when you've said no to somebody and given them instructions with the qualities of kindness, or you've stopped criticising or blaming another and started taking responsibility.

I attended a surf life-saving conference in New South Wales, and they shared survey results on what keeps volunteers devoting hours of their free time. The first need was autonomy – the ability to have a choice (which fits with our discussion on what people need in chapter 5, and the SCARF model). Nursing is the same. Nurses working in settings that support greater nurse autonomy are more satisfied with their jobs, experience less burnout, and desire to continue working in those hospitals. They also report great teamwork and better quality of care. Bonobo mode gives people choices to make a happy team and embodies the 'doing with' rather than 'doing to' delegation. You can do this by being curious and open after you have given an instruction.

You might not think you can provide a choice in some matters. I encourage you to think if you could give a couple of options. A simple choice is doing a task 'now or later'. Or, 'would you like to do it this way or that way?'

The first step to awakening your bonobo is acknowledging what is at stake if you don't change from being a cockatoo. Will you be more confident at work being a bonobo more often? What would it feel like to be a bonobo?

When you're stressed, take a breath and shift from the cockatoo. If you start blaming other people, ask yourself:

- Do I know the whole story?
- What am I missing?
- How can I gather more information?
- How can I express what I need to be done without intimidating my team?
- How can I modify my tone and facial expressions to show compassion?
- What changes can I make to build accountability in my team?
- How can I stay open to feedback and allow others to share their views?

Act and speak neutrally when you are in the bonobo identity. You have to come across as a drama-free zone, giving the impression they've shifted into a space where you are saying, 'I care about you and the rest of the team'. A drama-free zone is where you reframe *what we can't do* to *what we can*. Let's consider this example of a complaint about a teammate being behind in their work. You could say in a neutral tone, 'Sharon's behind with her work? What can we do to help?' If the teammate says, 'Billy is hopeless, and the quality project is a disaster,' you can reframe it to, 'Billy is the senior on our team, and the project didn't go as planned. Okay.'

Use your imagination to create that drama-free zone. Some of my clients like to imagine a bubble of white light around them. This bubble is their drama-free zone. One nurse leader simply named a clear space around her the 'professional zone' (she also included her head in that zone). She reminded herself of this zone before she answered the phone or had any conversation. Do what works for you.

Bonobo mode reduces reactivity by being less cocky and allowing the team to focus on what is important. In the past, the cockatoo, rather than the bonobo, has been modelled as how leadership looks. Acknowledge that your old selves are a well-worn path, and it will take a little practice to think, feel and act as the bonobo or the lion.

★ **Be more bonobo:** make the quality of your directions count towards increasing resources in others and the unit.

Guide dog the coach

The last dysfunctional nurse identity we give a countertype to is mumma bear (the nurturing parent/rescuer). This nurturer part makes you think you have to save people. Or be the hero for them. You over-care, over-give and often burn yourself out in the process. 'When I talk to managers, I feel they are important. When I talk to leaders, I get the feeling that I am important,' says Alexander den Heijer, an inspirational speaker whose mission is to help people flourish. Mumma bear loves helping and feels special doing so.

The fourth transformational nurse identity is the coach who helps you reduce stress, and enables self-responsibility and engagement with your teammates. The coach helps their teammates learn. Guide dog is our animal friend who makes a great coach. Guide dog is perfect to be the coach as they are humble, loyal animals that love to help but keep the owner safe by leading them around obstacles. The three keywords to remember with guide dog mode are essence, boundaries and responsibility.

- Essence:
  - gets to the heart of what is essential
  - has a good perspective
  - clearly defines their role and others' roles
  - is good at listening.

- Boundaries (for self and others):
  - gives no more or less than is asked
  - sees what their responsibility is and is not
  - has a growth mindset – the 'not yet' mindset
  - 'I can choose what I do'
  - 'we can work together'.

- Responsibility:
  - fosters engagement
  - asks for opinions
  - asks coaching questions
  - knows that empowering others is key
  - trusts others have what it takes.

The essence of this identity is teaching your team to fish rather than giving them a fish.

If you become mumma bear at times, acknowledge that what you do isn't selfless as you get to feel great for saving the day. Mumma bear also doesn't enable your team to think, and can lead to burnout for you. Asking others questions and being a coaching leader will increase their sense of responsibility and reduce your workload in the future. It also leads to succession planning.

Transformational leadership aspects of the coach (guide dog)

In Transformational Leadership, the building block for our coaching guide dog is 'individual consideration'. The leadership focuses on coaching and mentoring. This leader is aware of their team's needs and goals, and sees the intrinsic value in others. They use coaching questions and pause before they speak.

Tracey, a nurse leader I was coaching, had complaints from her team about her communication style. Adopting this guide dog identity improved her relationship with her team. She said that understanding the SCARF model was critical to her success as she kept the possibility of a status threat in mind before any conversation. Her strategy was to ask questions to improve the other's status. A surprising by-product was that this reduced her stress exponentially. Coming to work feels more relaxed now as she feels like she doesn't need to have all the answers. With some good questions for her teammates and fellow team leaders, she feels more supported and less alone 'at the top'. Another new nurse leader I know has high standards but wasn't sure how to communicate them. He said it was easier to do things himself. A divisional leader worries about him as she thinks he is on the road to burnout. A mumma (papa) bear that needs to learn how to coach and embody the guide dog.

Let's use surf life-saving as an example again. At a leadership conference for surf life-saving, I asked other presidents for advice. Nathan, the president of Wanda Surf Life Saving in Cronulla, New South Wales advised me to 'travel in pairs'. He said, 'With any new initiative, meet with members of your team and ask their advice. Ask who needs to be involved with this.' If you've got ideas, ask others good questions to help get them engaged with your project, so the responsibility isn't always on you.

When you 'travel in pairs', you get buy-in by asking others their opinions about your new initiative. It also means, like the new nurse leader, you're not doing everything yourself and burning out in the meantime. It is an easy trap to fall into when you want the results.

Asking good coaching questions takes time, and bonobo (challenger) is often needed on the floor to direct your team. However, a good coaching question can be powerful when leading your team on a shift. A simple question to get your team members to think about how to approach a patient could be, 'What is your priority with this patient today?'

It can be confusing to know when to use a particular identity. A coaching conversation is warranted if there are any emotions in the conversation. You will use the guide dog part when giving feedback or educating. Questions are helpful to get your team to think at any time.

A coaching model can be helpful when approaching a coaching conversation. Often, the unit's nurse manager gets to sit down and have significant conversations with the team. There's a model called GROW that's simple to use. It addresses goal, reality (what's happening now, the resources you do or don't have), options and will (what can you commit to and when?).

You don't need a model to ask good questions. Here are some coaching questions from Rose O. Sherman, nurse leadership author of the book *The Coaching Nurse Leader*:

- What solutions are you considering?
- What is the next action you can take in this situation?
- What evidence are you using to reach that conclusion?
- How do you know your assumptions are accurate?
- How will you know if the patient's condition is improving?

I also have some additional questions, this time from Michael Bungay Stanier's *The Coaching Habit: Say less, ask more & change the way you lead forever*:

- And what else?
- What's the real challenge for you here?
- How can I help?
- If you're saying yes to this, what are you saying no to?

It can be hard to break the habit of over-caring and rescuing. Have a mantra like the following, or make another one that makes sense to you:

- They are capable people.
- I can help by asking questions rather than providing all the answers.
- I can show them how to fish.

★ **Be more guide dog:** take your team to places in their thinking that they could not have gone on their own.

SHIFTING NURSE IDENTITIES

No one stays in any one identity. Adaptability is a crucial leadership skill. When I do coaching, I shift from guide dog when asking questions to bonobo when I need to create some healthy pressure, then to dolphin when I need people to explore and firm up goals and break them down into milestones. You can do the same. Don't overthink who you need to shift from and when. Once you get to know these parts and their functions, it will be easier.

There are many ways to shift parts: mindfulness, reflective pauses, coaching and insight. As children, we were taught to take a breath before we respond. In this case, you can take a thoughtful pause to reflect and switch to a more helpful part of you. You can ask yourself – what's needed here? Who do they need me to be – more lion (adult mode), or to get the job done and keep them happy and engaged? The thoughtful pause can also allow you to check who you are right now. Which nurse identity? Dysfunctional or transformational?

I use transformational chair work in my practice as a psychologist. The chair work is a fantastic process and brings enormous insight. This process has foundations in Gestalt therapy and voice dialogue. I start by letting the room represent the person as a whole, including the parts. The individual moves their chair around the room to speak from the different parts as I interview that part. I talk to the client in the third person, as I want them to understand that they are not that identity. It's just a part of them. Then once we have enough information from that part, we shift to another.

Nurse identities are a part of you

Let's use Paul as an example. When he goes to the nurse managers' meeting with the directors, he sits in the back and doesn't speak up. These are the questions I asked the part of him that behaves like this:

· When Paul goes to the meeting, are you the one that sits in the back?
· What do you say to Paul to get him to do this?
· How do you make Paul feel?
· How long have you been around for Paul?
· What purpose do you think you have for Paul in the meeting?

After shifting to other helpful and not-so-helpful parts, the individual feels more empowered to be able to move (without my help). Knowing you can move parts at will is empowering.

A shift in focus can also achieve changing into another identity. Shift to noticing another's strengths and you are bonobo the challenger or guide dog the coach. Shift to solutions focused and you are in dolphin the creator. Listen with sincerity and you are in guide dog. Connect to the reason for transforming yourself and you are in eagle the catalyst.

To start with, these additional transformational nurse identities may feel overwhelming. An antidote is to stay in the lion (adult) as it has the elements of these separate parts. These identities you have met in this chapter give richness to the lion part and illustrate how Transformational Leadership can be practical when used in this fun way.

This model also takes into account different strengths in your personality. You may be more comfortable in bonobo (challenger) than guide dog (coach). You can lead with the best part of you. The other identities can point to areas of leadership development. Knowing they're all lion means you aren't too far off with your leadership behaviour.

Know your triggers. Fill out this list in your leadership dashboard, so you can be aware of what you do and when.

- When a team member is in shock, I shift to _____ (nurse identity).
- When a team member is angry, I shift to _____ (nurse identity).
- When my team members are _____ I shift to _____ (nurse identity).

Look at where you could do a reflective pause. Notice who you are being. You can also do this with journaling. A great journal exercise is to write from each part. You will get to know these parts inside you at a deeper level.

It takes practice to become aware of who you're being. Seeing it in others is often easier, so start there and then shift to yourself. Watch the way you justify each part. Your mind will justify why you should stay in a dysfunctional nurse identity, such as cocky or mumma bear. Expect that, and don't fight it. Notice the excuses objectively. Objectivity means you are in lion and have not bought into what your mind is telling you.

CONCLUSION

This chapter introduced you to more characteristics of a great leader using transformational nurse identities. There is a great chance of being a transformational leader if you try to be an objective, present and authentic person. The ingredients for the adult mode that make you unleavable are the catalyst, creator, challenger and coach. You get to put them together in a recipe to escape the dysfunctional nursing identities that don't work into the ones that do – leaving the drama behind. Then you can pay attention to transforming your unit. Use the animal countertypes – dolphin, bonobo, guide dog and eagle – to help you distinguish between the identities and have fun with them. Stop focusing on the issues in people and yourself. Start focusing on how you can lead to keep your team in the parts that work the best. Keep in mind we want them in lion (adult mode) too to function at their best, so the more you can stay there, the more they will be in a bonding pattern that works for everyone:

- **Be more dolphin:** Think about possibilities and be open to the size of the solution not needing to equal the size of the problem.
- **Be more bonobo:** Make the quality of your directions count towards increasing resources in others and the unit.
- **Be more guide dog:** Take your team to places in their thinking that they could not have gone on their own.
- **Be more eagle:** Be courageous enough to light the way with vision and strategy.

The next chapter will explore how you can influence your work culture to create an adaptive team wanting to learn. You may have suspicions about the efficacy of feedback. You will discover a way of giving feedback that beats the old ways. This form of feedback will align better with your values and improve your relationships with your team rather than weaken them. And it puts an end to procrastination around this essential nurse leadership function.

8

Learn and grow

PROVIDING FEEDBACK IS A CRITICAL LEADERSHIP SKILL

To become accredited as a healthcare leadership coach, I had to interview 12 nurse leaders. It was unanimous: avoiding providing feedback was the number one leadership issue. Providing feedback will help your team learn, grow and improve. It happens between managers and your team, or even peer to peer. Nurse managers said they had no difficulty doing it. They stated they shared what to do and say with their leadership team, but admitted this often did not improve matters. In my experience, fear of wrecking relationships and the stress of giving feedback are why they shirk this essential task. Just thinking about giving feedback gave them anxiety.

They want an easy process to follow and to know the conversation isn't ruining the relationship. Performance conversations, including feedback, can be easy when you have a structure and approach it deliberately. The feedback can be formal, informal or digital. Formal could be a performance review or feedback from a particular event. Informal is in the flow of every day, and it's generally unplanned. Digital is online and can consist of a text or email. Some apps are currently being trialled to help this process.

When nurse leaders learn how to do this right, it improves much more than the level of patient care. I firmly believe everyone wants to do a great job. Not helping them to develop means you're robbing them of a means of fulfilment. Also, there is an impact on your leadership if you don't give feedback. Avoiding hard conversations reduces your confidence in your ability to lead. Learning how to have challenging discussions and then doing so increases confidence. Nothing better than the feeling after overcoming one of your fears! Not knowing how to have feedback conversations has been cited as a contributing cause in nursing burnout in nurse leaders. Surprisingly, doing it right builds relationships.

It's easier to learn than you think. One team I trained in how to give feedback, using the feedforward model I'll share with you in this chapter, went from a four-out-of-ten confidence in providing feedback to an eight to nine level of confidence after just a three-hour training session. To become a transformational leader, you must learn and practise this skill. Speaking from the transformational nurse identities will help you.

Feedback needs to be a two-way street. A culture change may need to occur, starting with you as leader. Daniel Goleman, author of *The New Leaders* and *Emotional Intelligence*, says leaders need to 'break through the information quarantine around them and the conspiracy to keep them pleased'. Leaders need to be open to receiving feedback as well.

In this chapter, we'll turn feedback on its head by linking it to the transformational nurse identities. You will learn about your responsibilities and cultivating a feedback culture. You'll discover how to come from a more helpful identity when you give feedback, and you will achieve a different outcome from your experiences with feedback in the past.

In this VUCA world, we need agility with learning. Charles Darwin, best known for evolutionary biology, said: 'It's not the strongest of the species nor the most intelligent that survives. It's the one that is most adaptable to change.' A structure can help build confidence in providing timely feedback that doesn't stress your team or the leader. In this chapter we'll outline such a system, and expose why the commonly used feedback sandwich doesn't work.

CREATING A POSITIVE, ENGAGED WORKFORCE

Feedback is giving your considered reactions to another's perfor-mance of a task. Performance conversations like this must happen daily as part of continuous improvement. It builds your team's capacity. A common trap when considering improving a team's performance is to focus on what is not done well. You can build competencies by acknowledging strengths. Positive reinforcement leads your team to relax into what they do well and focus on what they want to improve and eases their mind.

Positive feedback is critical and is the foundation that builds a confident workforce. Positive feedback can be commenting on strengths, successes and efforts. It reinforces the preferred behaviour, making it more likely to happen again, and patient care improves. You may recognise positive feedback from the language of appreciation in the workplace (chapter 4). It's words of affirmation that many nurses crave – especially the outgoing, talkative ones.

Be on the lookout for opportunities for positive reinforcement, especially if somebody is learning. Make sure it's sincere, and don't overdo it. When you are active listening, listen for strengths.

Be sure to make the positive affirmation meaningful. Link it to patient results or impact on the team. Give it as close as possible to the event and in front of others. Be specific and detailed in your praise to make it easier for them to repeat the behaviour. For example, 'Good pick up on the patient's foot changing colour and persevering when the resident didn't answer your first page – that's going to make all the difference.'

Remember the gap and gain we spoke about in chapter 3? Often new nurses will focus on how far they have to go and not how far they have come. Take advantage of any opportunity to focus on what they've learned to date. They will be surprised. You could also get them to list what they can do now that they couldn't do six months ago.

You might find it challenging to do this on the run. Don't overthink it, and do try to say it your way. If you often use the word 'love', feel free to say, 'I love that you did that'. If this is not you, say, 'Good on you for helping out', or you can be more formal if that's your thing. In your attempts to give positive feedback, be you.

You can be forgiven for thinking that too much positivity can feel fake. I am not talking about running around throwing flowers in the air and talking sunshine, unicorns and lollipops. I am pointing towards shifting your focus from concerns and faults to actively looking at what is going right or well in others – and then expressing it aloud to them. Don't be fake, but be aware that we are all more critical of ourselves than we will ever be of others. They often know what their gaps are (though not everyone does – some have a very high and dangerous view of their abilities).

WHY THE TRADITIONAL FEEDBACK SANDWICH DOESN'T WORK

The feedback sandwich is when a person gives constructive criticism between two positive statements about personal behaviour. For example: 'I think you're great, but you've not been timely with the vital signs. But you have an excellent rapport with the patients.' The feedback sandwich doesn't surprise anyone, and people can feel the 'yeah, but … ' coming on.

There is nothing wrong with objectively saying what you noticed. However, I will give you a better way to do this later in the chapter. Wrapping the criticism in the positives muddies the waters around the message, and the crucial factor is unclear. The positive points are also lost and even downplayed by the receiver, and the person doesn't feel valued. They won't hear the positive affirmation as they'll focus on the negative part. Also, the feedback sandwich focuses on that which can't be changed: past behaviour. You can only alter the future.

It would be best if you had your team become active participants in the learning process. Telling them what to do means they are passive, not developing their critical thinking. Psychologist Ian James researched the feedback sandwich but called it the sh*t sandwich. He discusses his conclusions on its effectiveness in the article 'The Rightful Demise of the Sh*t Sandwich: Providing effective feedback', published in *Behavioural and Cognitive Psychotherapy*. James suggests that feedback is a complex process, and methods that place an emphasis on the learner as an active participant in the learning process should be encouraged. The paper suggests that negative feedback should generally be avoided.

On the netball court, our coach told us what we were doing wrong and right during the breaks. We accepted this as part of netball culture, to receive input from the coach in this way. This same acceptance could come from an educator on the ward giving feedback. If a nurse is junior, they would expect input. But what happens when the nurse on the floor gets more senior? Does the expectation of feedback shift and the dynamic change? In my experience, it does. So even an educator would do well to find a better process that helps give feedback to improve performance.

The feedback sandwich may have been your go-to process in the past. Maybe you'll feel a bit lost now we have shown it isn't so helpful. Habits can be hard to break. Go easy on yourself. Try substituting with feedforward, the future and solutions-focused approach we discuss next.

Reflect on:

Self-awareness: Have you ever had a feedback sandwich? How did it feel, and where was your focus?

Stop doing the feedback sandwich or connecting criticism with a positive comment. The positive will get lost, and it will feel like you're trying to be nice to soften the critique. In chapter 1 we talked of putting deposits in the emotional bank account. You can create a positive feedback culture and ensure you have far more positive interactions than negative. It can be as simple as, 'I agree with that', or, 'that's a good idea'. Build a shared conversation of competencies and positivity that will cushion any potentially damaging conversations. It softens any criticism when the positives are scattered throughout the day. Then use the formula below as a new way to give feedback.

USING FEEDFORWARD

Feedforward is the best feedback model as it's forward and solutions focused. You are in guide dog (coach) mode when you use this approach. Sometimes you may have to engage other nurse identities, such as eagle (catalyst) or bonobo (challenger). Feedforward originated from the work of Marshall Goldsmith, a master coach recognised as one of the top 10 business thinkers in the world and a top-rated executive coach worldwide. He says feedback is limited, static and focused on past events, whereas feedforward is expansive and dynamic. Feedforward focuses on the best actions for next time.

I use feedforward because we can change the future, not the past. It has the same goal as feedback, which is improving below-par behaviour – but it's more constructive. Don't worry. It addresses what didn't go well, but we allow the team member to articulate what happened. It's more productive to help people be right than prove them wrong. It's more respectful, reduces their stress, and won't shatter their confidence. Then we concentrate on what could happen next time.

This type of feedback still sets the context around the behaviour. The difference is we ask the individual their version of events first. Asking them prevents a status threat. Next, ask what action they consider would be best next time the situation occurs, giving them autonomy and an opportunity to think. Your team does want to think for themselves and improve. When you allow the development to come from them, you are in the lion (adult mode) – 'I'm okay, you are okay'. Feedforward comes from the assumption your team can make positive changes.

People do not take the feedforward approach as personally as feedback. You'll find feedforward easier and less stressful to use than feedback as it maintains the relationship. Difficulties go into the background when you focus on solutions, and the future looks brighter for everyone.

'Imagining a future is the central organising function of the brain,' says Martin Seligman, the father of positive psychology. People love to think of what they can do well and plan for their future. Dr David Rock, who developed the SCARF model covered in chapter 5, says we respond to feedback about what we did wrong only one out of 13 times – so once out of 13 times sharing what somebody did wrong results in behaviour change! He says the mind goes into an ego-protective mode. It shifts to proving to ourselves and those around us that we're not sub-standard people rather than focusing on improving our behaviour. Feedforward focuses on what you can do next time rather than what you did wrong and so reduces defensiveness.

It may seem like you aren't addressing the error because it's not coming from you. Try thinking of it this way: you are offering the other person the first option to say what happened and provide their point of view. The goal is better performance and to keep them feeling respected, engaged and fulfilled. They are keeping their status intact. It will be less stressful for them if you ask what happened with an open mind. Pay attention to your facial expressions, tone of voice and body language. If you do this, they will keep the thinking part of their brain on (low stress) and be more motivated to change. They're initiating the learning and the growing and coming up with ideas about what they could do next time.

If they don't understand what they did wrong, you can ask permission: 'Is it okay if I share with you what I witnessed and ways I think you could improve?' Asking permission increases their autonomy, status and relatedness. It's like knocking on the door to their house and asking – can I come in? You wait to be invited in, you don't barge in the door. When they say yes, it increases the probability they will listen, consider and implement your suggestion. If you want to improve their openness, ask another question to give them more control and get another yes – such as: 'Is it okay to do it now?'

A 'yes set' is when you build an agreeable frame of mind. Erickson asserts that if you agree with statement number one, you are more likely to agree with statement number two. If you agree with statement number two, you will be more likely to agree with number three. Advertisers use this yes phenomenon as well. They offer a few truisms and link the following yes to their product; for example, 'you need to keep up to date with technology (we think yes) and you are too busy to research it yourself (yes) – this is how product x makes this easy for you (YES, I want in!)'.

Sometimes you don't have time to ask permission or ask them what happened. Being direct at times is perfectly fine – it's about context. Like at netball, we package feedback in a certain way. In an emergency or if you're too tight on time, you can say, 'Hey, do it like this.' Say it as bonobo, not the cockatoo. Your team will appreciate it. But when you do have time, use the feedforward model. It's a different context, and you can use a less direct approach.

Ensure you're in the empathetic lion (adult) mode before approaching these conversations. Think about what nursing identity you will need to get the job done. I go between bonobo (challenger) and guide dog (coach). Be gently assertive about your goal. Give autonomy and set the scene for certainty (SCARF model): 'Hi, I'd like to talk about what happened on Wednesday. Is now a good time? Or when would you like to meet?'

Ask them for their opinion of what happened, their part in it, or whatever is relevant. You can use these questions from the book *Crucial Conversations: Tools for talking when stakes are high*, by Joseph Greenny, Kerry Patterson, Ron McMillan, Al Switzler and Emily Gregory:

- How do you see it?
- What's your perspective?
- Can you help me understand?

Respond using active listening without your defences going up. Remember to stay neutral and reframe, as you learned in chapter 7. Remind yourself that you're going for a win–win. You want to keep their status and go into problem-solving with them. Discuss their actions in objective terms if they haven't stated them, and then describe the impact of those actions. Or ask them what they see the effect as. You're going into bonobo, the challenger, here, and the risk is you can come off as leading them. Take care when you ask a question. Again, think of the SCARF model; you are triggering relatedness and fairness reward responses. Listen again. See if they've got any ideas for the next time this situation occurs.

If they don't have any ideas about what they could do next time, ask if it's okay if you provide some suggestions. Then ask them what they think the next steps are and ask if there's anything you can do to help. Build an agreement and thank them for their willingness to have this tough conversation.

Let's talk about the impact – the why – behind having a conversation like this. Consider the possible outcomes if the behaviour doesn't change. For example, the reasons you need a feedback conversation might be evidence-based practice, infection control standards, economics, patient wellbeing or impact on others.

When starting a feedback conversation, remember they may not feel safe or want to have this discussion with you. The timing could be wrong, and psychological safety is why you must ask permission first. Accept what the nurse says even if they don't want to talk to you: 'Is it okay to talk about this now? If not, when would be a good time?' Asking this question increases a sense of autonomy according to the SCARF model. Actively listen. In the book *Crucial Conversations*, the authors say that in a high-stakes conversation you must make the conversation safe so you can talk about almost anything. To make it safe, show your good intent. Listen and make sure you are in non-reactive lion (adult) mode before the conversation. Show you care about them, and you care about what concerns them.

CREATING A LEARNING MINDSET AND CULTURE

You can encourage a learning mindset in the unit to promote growth. A learning mindset is about opening yourself up to development. No matter how experienced you are, a feedback culture is a way to foster a learning mindset in your team. The feedback culture must start with you. Understanding the natural responses to feedback allows you to ride the wave of resistance if it occurs.

The SARA model is a natural response to feedback:

- **Shock:** 'This can't be right.'

- **Anger:** 'Who said this?'
- **Resistance:** 'No one is perfect. That's the way I am, take it or leave it', or, 'It wasn't my fault'.
- **Acceptance:** 'How can I best use this feedback? What can I do? Who will help me?'

Reframing and understanding what is happening emotionally to you and your team mean wisdom and maturity enter the communication space. Knowledge of the ups and downs of emotions means you expect what is coming and don't get caught up in it. Unhooking from drama changes culture and your leadership style.

When you expect these responses, humanity and compassion arise and open you to a learning mindset. A learning mindset means we take ourselves less seriously and admit to mistakes. It means you, as a leader, will hear of near misses if you cultivate this development culture, reducing error cover ups. Being a role model for growth and an objective leader also improves the vibe in the unit.

You can be a role model for development and also have high standards about safety. A friend of mine is a director of nursing. Five years ago, she was a nurse unit manager in a general surgical ward. She is high functioning and task focused and expects her nurses to maintain high standards of patient care. She admitted that her team were too scared to come to her if they had an issue as they knew she had such high standards. They could tell she was annoyed and thought it wasn't good enough when a mistake was made. She realised this was a risk and worked on it with a coach outside the hospital. She didn't want to admit it to her divisional head, so she took care of it herself. Have high standards, but remember to soften your demeanour through being bonobo to increase patient and staff psychological safety.

In her book *Mindset*, Carol Dweck, an academic and researcher, named two kinds of students: 'know-it-all' and 'learn-it-all'. Know-it-alls are intelligent but aren't willing to challenge themselves lest they discover they aren't as bright as they thought. They're also scared they'll lose face with their peers or teachers. Learn-it-alls understand they don't know everything and believe if they don't understand something, it's just for now. They can learn. Know-it-alls compete with their peers, but learn-it-alls collaborate with them.

In a culture where knowledge is king, nurses risk being a bunch of know-it-alls. I know I was. I remember avoiding advanced resuscitation workshops while working part-time in the ICU, as I didn't want people to discover I'd forgotten things. I was in know-it-all mode. It was a protective function. Strange to consider, when I was so hard on myself. The reality was I couldn't have known all the answers. Who can? I was part-time, and everyone needs to refresh their knowledge. This avoidance made me lose confidence. I needed to do what Carol Dweck calls going into learn-it-all mode and think, 'I don't know it yet' – otherwise known as the 'not yet' or growth mindset.

We must also consider the language we use. Often we can create a drama-free zone by reframing a situation. Cy Wakeman, a drama researcher, author and speaker, gives a great example of how a leader can do this. She says, 'Three patients dumped on us' can become, with a reframe, 'Three new admissions'. 'ED dumped patients on us at a shift change' can become, 'ED is on surge protocol, and this is inconvenient for us because it's handover time'. No judgement, no drama, no continuing stories of us against them, which is a risk between wards.

Cy poses the question leaders can ask their team: 'Given it's shift change, what are your ideas to make this the safest and best experience for the patients?' She also encourages leaders not to buy into the drama. From my experience as a nurse and working with teams, I know there can be a lot of drama and defensiveness when people give you new admissions. I call it 'bed wars'. Those on the floor guard their beds, and the leaders above them are pleading for improved patient flow and empathy for the poor patient sitting in ED.

You might think if you show any vulnerability or say 'I'm learning', you'll lose face and be less trusted. I get that. Your team needs to trust you. But saving face and trying to be perfect and have all the answers can be exhausting. Being open to being wrong and trying to improve is more honest. If you don't know, don't pretend you do. Just say you will find out and will respond as soon as you can.

Another tip to reduce drama is to separate the *what* from the *who*. Don't allow your team to make uncompleted tasks personal. Make it about the behaviour, not the person. It's easy to create an 'in' group and an 'out' group by allowing people to make personal comments about others. It would be best if you were neutral.

You can also encourage a feedback culture by starting discussions with your manager. Ask your manager about your strengths and what they would like you to improve on. Then ask your team at the end of the shift, 'What could I have done better to make the shift easier for you? I'm open to feedback.' Then make sure you're open in lion mode without defences when you get the feedback. Normalise continuous improvement and personal and professional development in the unit by leading with your openness to change.

You might go into know-it-all mode and be scared to hear something less than glowing. That's normal, but remind yourself you never stop learning. It will get easier with practice, and you will get more courageous.

Feedforward principles summary:

1. Create a culture of positive feedback.
2. Create a feedback culture starting with you and encourage asking for it.
3. Ask permission before you give feedback or options or advice.
4. Be future focused.
5. Teach your team how to think.
6. Encourage and offer support.
7. Ask what their version of events is.
8. Ask what they would do if they had their time again.

CONCLUSION

You have transformed a critical leadership skill from a stressful task most leaders avoid to an empowering situation for everyone. Using positive statements and a feedforward approach will ensure performance in the team will rise, and patient safety and care will improve with fewer mistakes made. You and your team will be more open to learning. Errors will be easier to admit in the team due to enhancing the culture of learning and growth.

Stop thinking that as a leader you must have it all together and be in critical thinking mode in every situation. Start empowering your team members by remembering how their brain works and what you can do to ensure they can learn properly. Keep listening for strengths, using active listening to build a positive feedback culture.

In the next chapter, I'll introduce you to a new model of self-reflection, making it easy to be a transformational leader. This model will improve your confidence and exponentially increase the chance you will remember to be the type of leader you know your team needs. And, more importantly, one that you are proud to be.

9

Reflect forward

REFLECTING AND PLANNING

The British cycling team skyrocketed their success in an eight-year period by making a series of 1% performance improvements. Sir Dave Brailsford took them from mediocre to 16 gold medals in two Olympics and seven Tour de France wins using a theory of marginal gains. They improved a wide range of small things, such as painting the floor of the trucks that transported their bikes white so they could pick up on any dust affecting the bikes, and changing to lighter indoor racing suits. One intervention was to teach the riders to wash their hands to reduce the chance of catching a cold. Each slight shift wasn't enough on its own, but together they made a critical difference to performance. It became like a treasure hunt to find and solve minor issues.

You may have convinced yourself you need massive action to transform your units. It's easy to underestimate the impact of making minor improvements daily. If you improve 1% each day as a leader, or your ward's nursing care improves 1% each day, that means over a year you improve 37.78% (according to James Clear's calculations, author of *Atomic Habits*). In the beginning, there may not be much of a change, or you may not see a difference. But it won't be long before the law of compounding is evident and you will be witnessing massive improvements.

As a clinical leader, you need to evolve to improve care. You may have the best of intentions, but unless you keep who you need to be and what you need to do in the front of your mind, you won't succeed. You need a plan to engage and get high performance from your teams – to plan for the 1% shifts to see long-term changes. You also need a process to reflect so you can pivot when you notice you could do better.

Here are the four steps for reflecting and planning, which we explore in this chapter:

1. **Use future thinking.** Commit to who you want to be with a mental map.
2. **Reflect forward.** This is a simple process I'll outline for you which uses two simple questions. The first is about building on your success to build confidence, and help you quieten your mind. The second is about learning and planning.
3. **Build habits.** I'll introduce you to the when-then model and the if-then model. It's a simple way to build a habit and make it easy to remember what you need to do at any moment.
4. **Use reflective practices.** This can be formal and informal.

What we do daily is like compound interest and builds over time. It builds neural networks, which in turn produce a habit. With so much going on in healthcare and nursing, you need something that makes your life and evolving leadership easy. This simple process builds momentum and positivity and will help you get results.

Planning to succeed matters, and so does having a way to adjust the plan along the way. A method to adapt keeps you and your leadership relevant. 'And it does take courage to do something differently. To do something differently, you also need resilience because it doesn't always come to plan,' says Michael Bungay Stanier in *The Coaching Habit*.

In this book, we have spent time considering the past by acknowledging the impact of triggers. Your triggers may have you lost in drama and power struggles. Mindfulness is a gateway to connecting with others, a way to reduce stress, and it helps you respond rather than react.

We've also spent time looking at the future. A vision in nursing helps to motivate and put small things into perspective. In this chapter, we'll discuss a significant function of our mind: planning for the future. Planning to lead forward.

If you acted on chapter 4, you now have a vision for the future. It is easy to get despondent if your image doesn't come to pass. Often this happens because there isn't a plan attached to the vision. Confucius said, 'The man who moves a mountain begins by carrying away small stones.' Start with small actions in your plan that come from self-reflection, and use my reflect forward approach and then the if-then or when-then strategy.

Reflection aids strategy. Purposeful reflection is a tool that helps nurses gain self-knowledge and insight. It will guide your nursing practice to improve patient outcomes and problem-solving. Having an intentional reflective process also improves your confidence and your career progression. Rebecca, a clinical nurse specialist from a year-long leadership program, emailed me a week ago. She said the confidential reflective process and coaching helped her gain the confidence to fill in for a manager on holiday leave. By the end of this chapter, you will know which reflective practice will help you.

COMMITTING TO FUTURE THINKING

Let's look at the idea of a future self and how it can move you forward to your goal. You'll be drawn forward quickly to your destination if you're committed to it. Notable business consultant Kenneth Blanchard says, 'There's a difference between interest and commitment. When you're interested in doing something, you only do it when it's convenient. When you're committed to something, you accept no excuses – only results.'

In the feedback model – feedforward from chapter 8 – you help your team members anticipate and plan for future successes. You assist them in outlining what they would do next time. You can do the same for your leadership behaviours. Anticipate the future, visualise it and plan for success.

You may have underestimated how important anticipating the vision for your future is. Martin Seligman, the father of positive psychology, agrees. He and his fellow authors, Peter Railton, Roy Baumeister, and Chandra Sripada, say success comes from anticipating, rehearsing and evaluating future possibilities. They call it 'prospection'. They assert it guides your thoughts and actions, which is the cornerstone of success. This revolutionary way of thinking maintains that anticipated emotions can drive our behaviour instead of our feelings dragging us into drama (from pesky triggers).

That emotions guide our future is also mirrored in the work of Dr Joe Dispenza, who wrote *Breaking the Habit of Being Yourself*.

He uses walking meditations, where you walk as your future self – feeling the feelings of having already achieved your vision as if it has already happened. He says this creates the neural networks necessary to be that person. I think it reinforces an identity of being that person. Another fun process is Kylego, in which you talk excitedly about your future as if it's already happened. Comedian and transformational speaker Kyle Cease accidentally created it when driving to an audition with a friend. Kylego is an enjoyable, refreshing experience – great to get you out of lamb mode and into eagle the catalyst. I love using it in nursing masterclasses as it gives a fun, can-do vibe to a vision (perfect after lunch at a full-day training!).

Have you ever considered that you rarely act outside of your identity? For example, do you identify as a drinker? No? Then you won't buy alcohol. Do you identify yourself as a chocolate eater? Yes? Then you're more likely to buy chocolate (or struggle not to buy it).

'Identity change is necessary to change your actions,' says James Clear. Every action is a vote for who you are. A vote for what type of person you think you are. He says it's the deepest level of change. If you vote for being a transformational leader, you need your beliefs about yourself and others to align with that.

My dad Bill often quoted Henry Ford: 'Whether you think you can or you think you can't, you're right.' I'm pleased to have been brought up by a man who taught me the value of guarding your thinking and beliefs early on.

Rowena, a nurse educator, was having problems with a new fellow educator Ryan. She said he was relying on her too much and taking up time. Rowena's primary nurse identity was mumma bear – making herself always available and taking too much responsibility. She wanted high standards and got caught in a cycle of helping, then blaming him, and then feeling trapped as in lamb (victim). Taking sick days was a way for Rowena to have a break from the frustration. In our coaching, she resisted shifting to a transformational nurse identity as she said it wasn't in her nature to be assertive and confront the behaviour (bonobo). A few weeks later, Rowena made the shift when it hit home that the desired change in him had to come from her first. She has to be in lion mode (adult), and then he is more likely to take responsibility and shift there.

Anticipating the skills and emotions you'll need in the future allows you to rehearse and improve your confidence mentally. Think of Dr David Rock's SCARF model and how we like certainty in our lives. Making a mental model of a future action reduces stress. If we cultivate a map of our future, it's making a neural map for our minds to follow. Rowena used mental rehearsal. She practised out loud what she would say to Ryan.

Mental rehearsal is practising in your head for the future and is utilised by elite athletes for performance excellence. Mental rehearsal training was a successful workplace strategy for dealing with lateral violence in a hospital setting. New nurses learnt these skills to deal assertively with unwarranted behaviour. The results lasted at least a year after the skills were taught and practised. Martha Griffin conducted this study in 2004 and presented the 'ten most common forms of lateral violence'. I hear on many fronts that this sort of interpersonal issue occurs at all levels of nursing and creates unnecessary trauma and drama – railroading excellence in nursing care and nurses' wellbeing.

Nurses often think they must only think critically and use evidence-based practices. Using your imagination can be hard at work. Using your mind in this way can seem strange. You may even ask, 'Does it work?' It's working already, and you haven't noticed. The part of your brain called the reticular activating system is your security guard. You receive many bits of information from your senses; it has to filter some out. It shows you what it thinks is relevant or essential to you.

To understand how this works, consider when you last got a new car. Did you notice many vehicles of the same make and model as your car driving around? And you hadn't seen them before? You didn't have to try. Your mind filters out what is unnecessary to you and shows what you consider essential. The same happens when you keep what you want in the front of your mind. It shows you the path or the way to make it happen. You're in charge of how you programme your mind. You know you need to either search for the problem or the solution – for the person you want to be and the way forward. You can also use the filtering function of your mind when you are hypercritical of others. Be deliberate about looking for their strengths and what they do well. As I like to say, listen for strengths. Do it enough and your mind will catch up on what is important to you and start to look for it and show you.

Who do you want to commit to being? Go back to chapter 7 and decide if you want to be the catalyst, the creator, the challenger or the coach. Or perhaps you want to create your own transformational nurse identity? Todd Herman, author of *The Alter Ego Effect* and a global leader in peak performance, realised early in his career he had to take on a secret persona to take on the character traits he wanted. He says he has trained many elite athletes, entrepreneurs and entertainers, and they all do this. Like Bronte, a child protection worker. She wanted to be open, friendly, professional and an excellent mentor to her team, but didn't want to bring too much of herself to work. The goal was to protect herself. Working from an identity appealed to her, and she chose a guide dog to describe who she wanted to be. She loved the animal idea so much she started to name her boss a snake and her director a bulldog. Representing them as animals worked for her; she stated it depersonalised their behaviours, and they felt less harmful to her.

Who do you think you need to be? What behaviours do you need to make a priority? Keep them in mind for the next topic, where we're going to make a simple plan that connects the context with the action to get your desired outcome.

Dr Joe Dispenza says the starting point is to bring your visualisations to life by feeling you *are* that person. You can imagine yourself feeling the lion (adult mode) or one of the other identities. Make it meaningful to you. One of my nurse manager clients says the lion feels even but strong. Maintaining this is difficult for her with work pressures, so she focuses on softening her body. She reminds herself of what the lion thinks – we're all equal. She also likes thinking that the actions her team members take are just a part of them. The lion doesn't jump to conclusions, and gives people the benefit of the doubt. Then she reminds herself what a lion does – listens, but is assertive. She knows what it feels like to be a team player with a can-do attitude and what it feels like when she's not in the lion, and she's the cockatoo. You have to know what it feels like to you.

REFLECTING FORWARD

Reflect forward is an evolving framework for personal learning and development. It assesses your thoughts and actions to ensure you're moving towards your goals and vision. To reflect means to bend or look back. Reflecting forward is better, as you can't change the past. It enables you to plan what to do next, like feedforward. You can plan how to act next time.

Reflect forward consists of my two favourite self-reflective questions that I've used in different roles: supervision, coaching and training. I've used them with peer supporters, counsellors, psychologists, lawyers, managers of many other teams, CEOs, doctors, GPs and nurse leaders. They all like it because it works and is easy to remember.

The focus of reflecting forward is building your strength and capacity. It creates your knowledge of what you can do, and it plans for what's next. Reflect forward creates a humble knowledge platform to springboard you into your evolving leadership. The two simple questions are:

- What did you like about what you did?
- If you had your time again, what would you do next time? (There's always a next time.)

Having a process can be helpful. Reflect forward can allow you to plan for next time, using the vision you have of yourself. It's practical and keeps you in the lion (adult), where you are separate from judgements about yourself and others.

John Dewey was an education researcher and is often quoted as saying, 'We do not learn from experience ... we learn from reflecting on experience.' In searching for the source of this quote, I found his words on reflection from his 1933 book *How We Think:* ' ... learning includes the amassing and retention of information. But information is an undigested burden unless it is understood ... comprehension means that the various parts of the information acquired are grasped in their relations to one another'. He says constant reflection is needed to understand meaning, so amassing information is not enough. We considered this in chapter 2.

A study at Harvard Business School on the power of reflection had a random sample of 202 people. They gave each person an online creativity test. The instructions for the first group were to reflect on a pre-test of creativity, and then they were asked to write down any strategies they thought might be helpful for when they do the next test. Group two were also told to write down their plans but were advised that the researcher would share their notes with others. The third group watched or did the pre-test, but there were no instructions.

In the end, groups one and two performed significantly better than the control group, who had no instructions and didn't spend time thinking about the tasks. These results indicate that dedicating time to reflect on your work – with planning – affects performance.

The first part of reflect forward is a strength-based question. What did you like about what you did? It's noticing what you did well, which stimulates the neurotransmitter dopamine's release. This creates a positive reinforcer for that behaviour.

The second part of the question is based on research by Peter Gollwitzer, an accomplished researcher in behaviour change. He coined the term 'implementation intention'. Gollwitzer said a simple if-then plan significantly increases the likelihood of a new behaviour taking hold. We'll be going through the if-then plan soon.

You may already think you do reflective practice well. However, if you are honest, you will notice that most of us say to ourselves, *Oops, I'll never do that again.* My clients admitted they sometimes got stuck on self-judgement, and there is no honest self-reflection. They didn't have the learning 'not yet' mindset.

Be like a curious scientist in your life and treat trying the nurse identities as an experiment. It'll enable you to hold yourself and others lightly. Be compassionate and open to learning, adjusting and changing your hypothesis or assumptions about yourself and others.

Another way to prepare yourself is to reflect on who you need to be for the workday ahead. You can ask yourself, *what do I need to do to prepare myself to work at my best today?* You may need to keep checking, changing and pivoting with who you need to be. Can you say what transformational nurse identity you're in now? What do they all feel like to you? Notice what you did when you shifted from an ineffective nurse identity, such as the cockatoo (critical parent), to the bonobo (challenger). How did you make the shift?

You may get disheartened as you keep reverting, forget to plan, or you're not making the progress you're expecting. Planes and boats never go straight. They have to keep adjusting their course. You can also think of it as shifting gears on a car. Different gears are needed to get power at different speeds. I wrote this book, teach this stuff, and can still get caught in these dysfunctional and unhelpful identities. For instance, I can become too excited about an idea in mumma bear as I think I can do it all, and shifts to the cockatoo or even the hyena (rebellious teenager) when a judgement of others slips in. Then comes the lamb (adapted child/victim) when no one matches my excitement, and I start feeling helpless.

I expect this to happen now – and so should you. I plan for these moments with an if-then statement, which you will learn about shortly.

SHIFTING PLANNING INTO ACTION

A habit is a series of behaviours encoded in your brain. We know it's hard to change a pattern. There's an apt Hindu proverb: 'For the first 30 years of your life you make habits. For the last 30 years of your life your habits make you.'

Habits free up brain power by shifting the behaviour from system two thinking (conscious thoughts) into system one thinking (automatic thoughts). We can make the new transformational leader behaviours easy to remember with an if-then or a when-then statement. These statements contain the cues to do the desired behaviour. Keeping this simple frees up brain power and creates habits.

A when-then statement is for an event that happens daily, and you can plan a strategy. For example:

- When I go to work in the morning, then I remind myself who I need to be for the day.
- When I start a meeting with my team, then I do the acknowledgment of country.
- When I start the team meeting, then I thank everybody warmly for coming.

You can use other daily occurrences such as before you walk into work, talking to a particular person, handovers, allocating a new patient, and asking for volunteers.

For the if-then, an internal marker can be used. An internal marker is an emotion or thought. Like when you're noticing you're getting annoyed with somebody, when you see you're talking too much or when you're thinking, *what's the use?* These 'ifs' trigger your plan.

For example:

- If I get annoyed, then I will take a breath and compose myself.
- If I start talking too much, then I will take a breath and ask a question.
- If I have the thought *what's the use*, then I shift to the dolphin and start to think about how it can work.
- If I get frustrated with someone, then I will take a breath and ask myself what assumptions I have.
- If I start to give too many instructions, then I will take a breath and ask others what they think.

Try it for yourself:

- If [what you want to change] then [what you will do].

Using these two strategies is called an 'implementation intention'. Thinking about if-then helps you with thinking on the run. Often you can't make complex choices about who you need to be in the moment. It can also prevent overthinking and procrastination.

Much of the research by Gollwitzer on implementation intentions finds that if-then increases the success of many new habits. He calls it a 'miracle statement' as it overcomes many problems experienced when people go for new goals but stick to current routines. If-then statements have helped change behaviours ranging from changing recycling to improving weight loss or confidence, reducing stress and sports performance.

The new behaviour can feel overwhelming to remember to do. If-then and when-then tools increase the odds in your favour. It's a perfect tool for the busy mind as it's simple and energy efficient.

Consistency will always be the issue with a new habit, so you can buddy up with somebody or get some coaching. You can also plan for the obstacles.

You can use an if-then statement for the obstacles. Write the if-then statements on a card and keep it in your wallet. You could also put them in the notes section on your phone. If you lose the courage to act differently, remind yourself what's at stake. Keep the process simple and make the *if* and the *then* specific and doable. And only plan for a couple at a time, till they are ingrained – and then plan for more!

PLANNING TO SUCCEED IN A PROJECT

Time to go deeper into the planning process. Start with thinking about the target you wish to meet. Is it to get a champion for some projects, or is it to build confidence in your new team members? Ask yourself:

- Why is it important?
- Why now?
- What is possible if you meet this target?
- What happens if you don't meet it?
- What behaviours are getting in the way?

Think of the dysfunctional nurse identities. What new behaviours do you need or who do you need to be to meet this outcome? Go back to chapter 7 if you need some inspiration. Which behaviour would cause a domino effect with the others or make the most sense to start with?

REFLECTION NEEDS AN EVOLVING PROCESS

At age 33, Australian Rachael Robertson was Antarctica's second woman expedition leader. She found journalling in that intense year-long leadership role was a powerful way to reflect, learn and gain perspective. She wrote about her journey in an engaging book called *Leading on the Edge*. Leadership is a process, not a role, so your reflection must be consistent and evolving. You can use formal or informal methods. If you're ad hoc with your leadership, it means you aren't taking your leadership role seriously or you're not committed to the results you want.

I've run several workshops on reflective practice. Some formal methods – like Gibbs's reflection process and Borton's model – can be used (I have provided links in the references). These are great models in a traditional setting like group coaching, or if you run reflective practice groups yourself.

If you're going to use these in your group, my tip is to use them for positive behaviours first. Focusing on positive behaviour is a way to build trust in a new group. I find group coaching helpful, and so do my clients. You surround yourself with people who are like you and want improvement. You engage in positive, solution-focused discussions.

Choose your company wisely. Being around positive, growth-oriented people is a way to support your growth and development. I walk with a fellow business owner, coach and trainer once weekly, and we both feel like it's our upbeat tune-up. Jim Rohn, a renowned entrepreneur, business coach, motivational speaker and author, says you are the average of the five people you spend the most time with. What would that average look like for you?

The Sunshine Coast University Hospital has participated in a study using reflective practice to improve their critical thinking. They also wanted to support their people, build team cohesion, and help reduce their nurse workers' stress and compassion fatigue. Their reflective practice group supports their team with nursing and caring interpersonal aspects. A supportive group environment is a positive way to navigate complex clinical and leadership issues. Other reflective practice processes, like 360-degree feedback, can help give you insights, as a leader, into your strengths and gaps in competencies. Having several different ways to reflect can mean you can find something that works for you and your leadership team.

My friend Bernadette worked most of her career in the Emergency Department before she studied midwifery. She said that she and her team experienced hundreds of extreme traumas over the years in ED. They had to keep going each shift. She thought the traumas didn't affect her. When she started midwifery, an old story rose in her mind, like clockwork, once a week. Her mind replayed the details of the traumatic experiences until they disappeared. Then she was able to let it go. She said she did notice it mindfully, although she often became emotional and sometimes got caught up in her intense feelings.

In my experience as a psychologist, a reflective practice would've helped her process this at the time. She agrees, although she also admits, at the time, she would've thought it was useless. She and her team had thought they were coping and dealing with it.

A nurse leader I work with initially thought it would be hard to be 'real' in a group. Studies by Chris Dawber and Tom O'Brien in 2014 found otherwise. They did a longitudinal study of positive reflective practice groups in ICU and oncology. The participants reported a positive shift in trust, respect and feelings of safety.

It can be hard to imagine a reflective process as beneficial when you feel you've succeeded without one. There's never a wrong time to use reflective practice; however, formal methods can take time and can be complicated. This is why I introduced the simple two-step approach you can use at the end of the day or in any situation:

- What did you do that you liked?
- If you had your time again, what would you do differently?

Trial reflective group coaching in your leadership team. There are many ways to do this. You can use these two questions to reflect forward. You could have a book club where you discuss leadership books.[1] Another way you can have a leadership group reflective practice is using the leadership dashboard. I use this in my leadership workshops. You have access to the dashboard in chapter 3 and you're welcome to use it and start your own practice. Or you can use creative approaches to activate a more holistic view of your actions.

Some of my clients love strength cards or self-care cards. Even animal wisdom cards or angel cards might appeal to different people. We use them to invoke insight and discussion about what a card represents. It's a great way to get you out of your logical mind and open you up to a new perspective.

You can also use roleplay in reflective practice time to practise skills. Use the power of mental rehearsal to create neural networks to make it easier for you to do an action when the time comes. You can do your practice at home as well. Imagine yourself in the moment, having feelings and even moving your body as you would if you were doing that action or having that conversation with another person.

---

1   If you feel you don't have time to read regularly, you can also try a book summary app. I use one called Blinkist, but there are others around. Or you could use this book and take a couple of chapters at a time.

Valuing curiosity can be difficult when nurses value evidence-based practice. Remember how, a short while ago, smoking was allowed on the balconies in wards? I remember smoke billowing through into the ward when in front of me was a patient on oxygen. A sign said, 'Do not smoke. Oxygen in use.' What is set in stone today and accepted without question could be tomorrow's smoking in the wards (or even smoking in the nurses' station).

CONCLUSION

Reflection is a process in which you learn and grow. You must plan to grow and evolve, not leave it to chance. This is how you will revolutionise your leadership. Shifting who you think you are will also change how you see others. It's a game changer in making you more transformational. In this chapter, you've learned to simplify the process with two simple questions and the if-then and when-then approach that makes taking action easy.

Stop thinking a reflective practice is for clinical practice and accept it's also for leadership. There is a Chinese proverb: 'The best time to plant a tree was 20 years ago. The second best time is now.' It's never too late to do the little things that make the difference. Now is the time to start being who you need to be and use reflective practice to lead others.

Now it's time to summarise what you have learnt and think about the next steps.

Leadership is inside-out

Leading from the right part of you will transform you. As leadership is an inside-out job, you will lift your team to another level when you focus on the shift. Once you understand the theory of parts, you'll be a transformative and unleaveable leader. The four parts that are most dysfunctional are cockatoo, mumma bear, lamb and hyena. There's always defensiveness and a power struggle in these parts. The transformative parts are lion, dolphin, eagle, guide dog and bonobo. They are wise, inclusive and collaborative solution seekers.

You have the skills to help yourself and your team gain confidence, perform and learn with the evolutionary feedforward and reflect forward processes. Imagine six months from now, when you walk confidently into the unit. You're so self-assured because you can handle whatever comes at you, no matter the chaos in the system. You know that you will find within yourself the right part to address every leadership challenge. Your team is looking up to you. They're laughing and relaxed as they know you have their back.

Not only has your work life improved, but your home and personal relationships have also blossomed.

Cutting out drama and operating from presence will also give you the composure you need to make better decisions. You know what your team wants and are confident you know who you need to be to help them. The nurse leaders who I see do this are lit from within and feel more hopeful about their leadership and the future of healthcare. They are astonished at how fast they get promoted and how easy it is to champion projects that make a difference, and they are less stressed.

The journey to a transformational leader that revolutionises their own leadership and that of nursing is a shift in identity, focus, actions and understanding. It about being soft on people and firm with outcomes and standards. It's about deciding to operate at a high level and master both clinical and leadership skills. It may be challenging to maintain this due to a highly stressed, reactive and political environment. The notion of being a transformational leader may feel far from reality. Reframe this from a reason to stop trying to a reason for persisting. Having a positive focus that you can control – yourself – can be an anchor in the stormy seas ahead. Keep your eyes open for a way out, and then take your team with you. Be the pathfinder.

It can feel egotistical to aspire to be a transformational leader. But what is the alternative? A dysfunctional, leavable leader? Remember what Marianne Williamson wrote in *A Return to Love*:

> *Our deepest fear is not that we are inadequate. Our deepest fear is that we are powerful beyond measure. It is our light, not our darkness that most frightens us ... Your playing small does not*

serve the world. There is nothing enlightened about shrinking so that other people won't feel insecure around you.

Taking the time to hone your craft is an act of generosity for the patients you care for and the team you lead. Each time you opt out of drama and politics in the ward, it is a win for your team, patients and families, and even the community. Transforming yourself in healthcare happens one decision and if-then at a time. You must be deliberate, choose the right actions, surround yourself with likeminded people and work from the conscious transformational parts inside yourself.

Transforming nursing and your leadership is an inside job. The insights on who to be and what actions to take to get the right results can be difficult to keep consistent. I help guide leaders through this journey – a journey I've been on myself and am still travelling. I've seen hundreds of nurse leaders change themselves, their teams and their workplaces. All nurse leaders can arrive at this place, have a huge impact and be transformative leaders.

I am hoping you will come with me on this journey. Do what I say in this book, and if you want help, contact me to work with you. Helping make these concepts easy is what I do – I coach and train leaders to feel lighter, more hopeful and transformational. It's my mission to help positively transform healthcare.

If you are a leader and struggling to find a way to be the leader you want to be, I get it. My wish for you is that you find a way to surround yourself with trailblazers in healthcare, that you love your work, that you find the parts of yourself that are the ideal parts from which to lead, and that those who work with you feel privileged to have you lead the way.

References

(in order of appearance)

CHAPTER 1

Smallwood N, Karimi L, Bismark M, Putland M, Johnson D, Dharmage SC, Barson E, Atkin N, Long C, Ng I, Holland A, Munro JE, Thevarajan I, Moore C, McGillion A, Sandford D, Willis K. High levels of psychosocial distress among Australian frontline healthcare workers during the COVID-19 pandemic: a cross-sectional survey. Gen Psychiatr. 2021 Sep 6;34(5):e100577. doi: 10.1136/gpsych-2021-100577. PMID: 34514332; PMCID: PMC8423519.

Smallwood N, Willis K. 'Mental health among healthcare workers during the COVID-19 pandemic'. *Respirology*. 2021;26:1016–7. https://doi.org/10.1111/resp.14143.

Dobson, H., Malpas, C. B., Burrell, A. J. C., Gurvich, C., Chen, L., Kulkarni, J., & Winton-Brown, T. (2021). 'Burnout and psychological distress amongst Australian healthcare workers during the COVID-19 pandemic'. *Australasian Psychiatry*, 29(1), 26-30. https://doi.org/10.1177/1039856220965045.

Yerkes, R. M., & Dodson, J. D. (1908). 'The relation of strength of stimulus to rapidity of habit-formation'. Punishment: Issues and experiments, 27-41.

Arnsten AF. 'Stress signalling pathways that impair prefrontal cortex structure and function'. Nat Rev Neurosci. 2009 Jun;10(6):410-22. doi: 10.1038/nrn2648. PMID: 19455173; PMCID: PMC2907136.

Incredible Health: 'Study: 34% of nurses plan to leave their current role by the end of 2022'. IH-COVID-19-2022-Summary-1.pdf (incrediblehealth.com).

'Nursing in crisis: Hospital IQ survey highlights significant patient care challenges due to hospital staffing shortages'. Hospital IQ (hospiq.com).

Buchan, J., Catton, H., Shaffer, F. A. (2022) 'The Global nursing workforce and the covid-19 pandemic'. *Sustain and Retain in 2022 and Beyond.* (icn.ch).

Ayalew, E., Workineh, Y. 'Nurses' intention to leave their job and associated factors in Bahir Dar, Amhara Region, Ethiopia, 2017'. *BMC Nurs* 19, 46 (2020). https://doi.org/10.1186/s12912-020-00439-5.

Ghost Town, 2008. Spyglass Entertainment.

O'Sullivan, T., Green, T, Gillies, E. 'The Science of Self™ Accreditation Reference manual. 2020.

Losada M, Heaphy E. 'The Role of Positivity and Connectivity in the Performance of Business Teams: A Nonlinear Dynamics Model'. *American Behavioral Scientist.* 2004;47(6):740-765. doi:10.1177/0002764203260208.

Bennis, W. Nanus, B. *Leaders: Strategies for taking charge.* 2012. Harper Collins.

Kok, J., van den Heuvel, S. C (editors). 2019. 'Leading in a VUCA world: Integrating leadership, discernment and spirituality'. *Contributions to Management Science.* Springer Open. https://doi. org/10.1007/978-3-319-98884-9.

Zeldin, T. Conversation: *How Talk Can Change Our Lives.* 2000. Hidden Spring.

'A guide to the joint commission's communication goal: Improving the effectiveness of communication among caregivers'. (spok. com).

Bell, V., Wade, D. 'Mental health of clinical staff working in high-risk epidemic and pandemic health emergencies a rapid review of the evidence and living meta-analysis'. *Soc Psychiatry Psychiatr Epidemiol* 56, 1–11 (2021). https://doi.org/10.1007/ s00127-020-01990-x.

Florida, R. *The Rise of the Creative Class.* 2002. Wiley.

Dempsey C, Reilly BA. 'Nurse Engagement: What are the Contributing Factors for Success?' *J Issues Nurs.* 2016 Jan 31;21(1):2. doi: 10.3912/OJIN.Vol21No01Man02. PMID: 27853182.

Mercurio, Z. *The Invisible Leader: Transform your life, work and organization with the power of authentic purpose.* 2017. Advantage.

Arianna Huffington on the great resignation. Bloomberg.

Carnegie, D. *How to Win Friends and Influence People.* 1936. Simon & Schuster.

Rock, D. *Your brain at work: Strategies for overcoming distraction, regaining focus, and working smarter all day long.* 2009. Harper Business.

Broome, M.E., Sorensen Marshall, E (editors). *Transformational Leadership in Nursing: From expert clinician to influential leader.* Springer Publishing.

Casida J, Parker J. 'Staff nurse perceptions of nurse manager leadership styles and outcomes'. *J Nurs Manag.* 2011 May;19(4):478-86. doi: 10.1111/j.1365-2834.2011.01252.x. Epub 2011 Apr 25. PMID: 21569144.

'HILCA Accredited Practitioner workbook'. Datadrivesinsight.com.

Hersey, P. and Blanchard, K.H. (1969) *Management of Organizational Behavior: Utilizing Human Resources.* Prentice Hall.

Western, S. *Leadership: A Critical Text*, 3rd edition. 2019. Sage.

Eurich, T. 'Increase your self-awareness with one simple fix'. TED Talk.

CHAPTER 2

Goldsmith, M. *What Got You Here Won't Get You There: How successful people become even more successful.* 2007. Hachette.

Goleman, D. *Emotional Intelligence: Why it can matter more than IQ.* 1996. Bloomsbury.

Goleman, D., Boyatzis, R. Mckee, A. *The New Leaders: Transforming the art of leadership into the science of results.* 2002. Timewarner paperbacks.

Spano-Szekely L, Quinn Griffin MT, Clavelle J, Fitzpatrick JJ. 'Emotional Intelligence and Transformational Leadership in Nurse Managers'. *J Nurs Adm.* 2016 Feb;46(2):101-8. doi: 10.1097/NNA.0000000000000303. PMID: 26796823.

Bass, B.M., & Riggio, R.E. (2006). *Transformational leadership* 2nd ed. Mahwah, N.J.: L. Erlbaum Associates.

Sherman, R. O. *The Nurse Leader Coach: Become the boss no one wants to leave.* 2019.

O'sullivan, T. Green, T. Gillies, E. 'The Science of Self Accreditation Manual'. TTI success insights.

Dixon-Woods M, Baker R, Charles K, Dawson J, Jerzembek G, Martin G, McCarthy I, McKee L, Minion J, Ozieranski P, Willars J, Wilkie P, West M. 'Culture and behaviour in the English National Health Service: overview of lessons from a large multimethod study'. *BMJ Qual Saf.* 2014 Feb;23(2):106-15. doi: 10.1136/bmjqs-2013-001947. Epub 2013 Sep 9. PMID: 24019507; PMCID: PMC3913222.

Online etymology dictionary.

Echevarria IM, Patterson BJ, Krouse A. 'Predictors of transformational leadership of nurse managers'. *J Nurs Manag.* 2017 Apr;25(3):167-175. doi: 10.1111/jonm.12452. Epub 2016 Dec 1. PMID: 27910229.

Western, S. *Leadership: A Critical Text*, 3rd edition. 2019. Sage.

Johansen, Mary L. PhD, RN, NE-BC. 'Keeping the peace: Conflict management strategies for nurse managers'. *Nursing Management* (Springhouse): February 2012, Volume 43, Issue 2, p 50-54, doi: 10.1097/01.NUMA.0000410920.90831.96

Harris, T. A. *I'm OK–You're OK. Climb out of the cellar of your mind.* 1972. Pan.

Kahnerman, D. *Thinking Fast and Thinking Slow.* 2012. Farrar, Straus and Giroux.

Dewey, J. *How We Think.* 1910. Dover Publications.

Unconscious bias test, Harvard.

CHAPTER 3

Avolio, B. j., Gardner, W.L. 'Authentic leadership development: Getting to the root of positive forms of leadership'. 2005, *The Leadership Quarterly* 16, 315-338.

'Cognitive Distortions: 10 Examples of Distorted Thinking'. (healthline.com).

Federn, Ego States, Encyclopedia.com.

Inside Out, Pixar.

Sky, J. *The Many Parts of You*. 2012.

Stone, H. Winkeman, S. *Embracing Ourselves: The voice dialogue manual*. 1989. New world library, San Rafael, California.

Vallacher, R.R, Nowak, A., Froehlich, M, Rockloff M. 'The Dynamics of Self-Evaluation'. *Personality and Social Psychology Review*. 2002;6(4):370-379. doi:10.1207/S15327957PSPR0604_11.

Andrew Neitlich, Idea of the leadership dashboard, Center for Executive Coaching.

Sullivan, D., Hardy, B. *The Gap or the Gain*. 2021. Hay House Business.

CHAPTER 4

'Better never stops: The road to real results with Virginia Mason Institutes approach for Health care improvement'. https://assets.asccommunications.com/whitepapers/virginia-mason-institute-wp-january-2022.pdf

Maurits, E.E., E de Veer, A. J., van der Hoek, L. S., L., & Francke, A.L. (2015). 'Factors associated with the self-perceived ability of nursing staff to remain working until retirement: a questionnaire survey'. *BMC Health Serv Res*, 2(15). DOI: 10.1186/ s12913-015-1006-x.

Lai J, Ma S, Wang Y, Cai Z, Hu J, Wei N, Wu J, Du H, Chen T, Li R, Tan H, Kang L, Yao L, Huang M, Wang H, Wang G, Liu Z, Hu S. 'Factors Associated With Mental Health Outcomes Among Health Care Workers Exposed to Coronavirus Disease 2019'. *JAMA Netw Open*. 2020 Mar 2;3(3):e203976. doi: 10.1001/ jamanetworkopen.2020.3976. PMID: 32202646; PMCID: PMC7090843.

Senge, P.M, *The Fifth Discipline: The art and practice of the learning organisation*. 2006. Crown business.

Gregory CS. 'Creating a vision for a nursing unit'. *Nurs Manage*. 1995 Jan;26(1):38, 40-1. PMID: 7898810.

Gregersen, H. 'Better brainstorming: focusing on questions, not answers for breakthrough insights'. *Harvard Business Review*. (hbr.org).

Vision story of the cathedral: 'Christopher Wren teaches how your attitude affects your results', Teach the Soul.

Gilbert, P. (2014) 'The origins and nature of compassion focused therapy'. *British Journal of Clinical Psychology*, 53(1), 6-4.

West, M. A. 2021. *Compassionate Leadership: Sustaining wisdom, humanity and presence in health can social care*. The Swirling Leaf Press.

Hougaard, R. Carter, J. Hobson, N. 'Compassionate leadership is necessary – but not sufficient'. *Harvard Business Review*. 2020 (hbr.org).

de Zulueta PC. 'Developing Compassionate Leadership in Health Care: An integrative review'. *J Healthc Leadersh.* 2015 Dec 18;8:1-10. doi: 10.2147/JHL.S93724. PMID: 29355200; PMCID: PMC5741000.

Baguley SI, Dev V, Fernando AT, Consedine NS. 'How Do Health Professionals Maintain Compassion Over Time? Insights From a Study of Compassion in Health'. *Front Psychol.* 2020 Dec 29;11:564554. doi: 10.3389/fpsyg.2020.564554. PMID: 33447247; PMCID: PMC7802760.

Kabat-Zinn, J. *Falling Awake: How to practice mindfulness in everyday life.* 2018. Little Brown.

Joh Kabat-Zinn: Defining Mindfulness: What is mindfulness? (mindful.org/jon-kabat-zinn-defining-mindfulness).

C4 consultancy website. Leaf on a stream recording. Resources – C4 Consultancy.

Neff, K. Definition and Three Elements of Self Compassion. (self-compassion.org).

Chapman, G. 1992. *The Five Love Languages: How to express heartfelt commitment to your mate.* Northfield publishing.

Chapman, G. White, P. 2012. *The Five languages of appreciation in the workplace: Empowering organisations by encouraging people.* Northfield publishing.

Yeager, V. A., & Wisniewski, J. M. (2017). 'Factors That Influence the Recruitment and Retention of Nurses in Public Health Agencies'. *Public Health Reports* (1974-), 132(5), 556–562. https://www.jstor.org/stable/26374167.

Chamanga E, Dyson J, Loke J, McKeown E. 'Factors Influencing the Recruitment and Retention of Registered Nurses in Adult Community Nursing Services: An integrative literature review'. *Prim Health Care Res Dev.* 2020 Sep 11;21:e31. doi: 10.1017/ S1463423620000353. PMID: 32912372; PMCID: PMC7503170.

Rosenthal experiment 2. Robert Rosenthal Study.

CHAPTER 5

Ziglar, Z. *See You At The Top.* 1986. Nightingale Conant Corp.

Hughes, R., Ginnett, R. Curphy, G. *Leadership: Enhancing the lessons of experience.* 2022. McGraw Hill.

Rock, D. *Your Brain at Work: Strategies for overcoming distraction, regaining focus, and working smarter all day long.* 2009. Harper Business.

Harris, T. A. *I'm OK–You're OK. Climb out of the cellar of your mind.* 1972. Pan.

Karpman, S. (1968). 'Fairy tales and script drama analysis'. *Transactional Analysis Bulletin,* 7(26).

Further explanations of Drama triangle. The Official Site of the Karpman Drama Triangle.

Don't be a Wally With Water. 1986. YouTube.

Norm Let Sleeping Norms lie, says irate widow of Life. Be In It artist. (theage.com.au).

Andrew Neitlich, The Best Executive Coaching Certification Program for 2022, Center for Executive Coaching.

Studies for Matthew Lieberman, as seen in Rock, D. pg 113-115. *Your brain at work: Strategies for overcoming distraction, regaining focus, and working smarter all day long.* 2009. Harper Business.

Gordon, E. 'Safety as the Brain's #1 Priority'. (thriveglobal.com).

Rock, D. 'Managing with the Brain in Mind by David Rock'. Academia.edu.

SCARF assessment: The NLI SCARF® Assessment. NeuroLeadership Institute.

CHAPTER 6

Hyatt, M. Quote by Michael Hyatt: 'How we lead ourselves in life impacts how we le ... ' (goodreads.com).

Carnegie, D. Quote by Dale Carnegie: 'People rarely succeed unless they have fun in w ... ' (goodreads.com).

Shah M. 'Impact of Interpersonal Conflict in Health Care Setting on Patient Care: The role of nursing leadership style on resolving the conflict'. *Nurse Care Open Acces J.* 2017;2(2):44-46. DOI: 10.15406/ncoaj.2017.02.00031.

Noone, C., Bunting, B. Hogan, M. J. (2005) 'Does Mindfulness Enhance Critical Thinking? Evidence for the mediating effects of executive functioning in the relationship between mindfulness and critical thinking'. *Frontline Psychology*, 6:2043. Published online 2016 Jan 19. doi: 10.3389/fpsyg.2015.02043.

Berne, E. 1964. *Games People Play.* Ballantine books.

McLeod, S. 2017. The Milligram Shock Experiment. Milgram Experiment: Summary, Results, Conclusion, & Ethics (simplypsychology.org).

Obedience to Authority, Yale University Library.

Cherry, K, 2021, The Stanford Prison Experiment. Zimbardo's Famous Study. (verywellmind.com).

Gross, James J. 2014. *Handbook of Emotion Regulation.* Guilford.

Summaries and Essays. Aaron Beck's Cognitive Behavioral Theory Essay. (novelsummary.com).

Psychology Tools Cognitive Distortions: Unhelpful Thinking Habits. Psychology Tools.

Yates, B. Tap with Brad.

Marston, W. M. 1929. *The Emotions of Normal People*. Read & Co. Science.

Free DiSC profile. https://www.123test.com/disc-personality-test/.

Sapolsky, R. 2017. *Why Your Brain Hates Other People*. (scribd.com).

CHAPTER 7

Dag Hammarskjöld Biography. (nobelprize.org).

Countertype definition and meaning. (collinsdictionary.com).

Choy A. 'The Winner's Triangle'. *Transactional Analysis Journal*. 1990;20(1):40-46. doi:10.1177/036215379002000105.

Bass, B. M., (1995) 'Theory of Transformational Leadership Redux'. *Leadership Quarterly*, 6(4), 463-478. Bass 1995 Transformational Theory [546g6e70ywn8] (idoc.pub).

Kashdan, T.B., & Rottenberg, J. (2010). 'Psychological Flexibility as a Fundamental Aspect of Health'. *Clinical psychology review*, 30 7, 865-78.

DeBono, E. 2004. *How to Have a Beautiful Mind*. Vermilion.

Robins, S. (2021). *Ducks in a Row: Health care reimagined*.

Wolpert, S. 'Putting Feelings Into Words Produces Therapeutic Effects in the Brain'. UCLA Neuroimaging Study Supports Ancient Buddhist Teachings. UCLA.

Tolle, E. *The Power of Now: A guide to spiritual enlightenment*. 1997.

Tolle, E. *Practising the Power of Now: Essential teachings, meditations and exercises for living the liberated life.* 2004. Hodder.

Pert, C. *Molecules of Emotion: The science behind mind-body medicine.* 1997. Simon & Schuster.

Broome, M. E., Sorensen Marshall, E. (editors). *Transformational Leadership in Nursing: From expert clinician to influential leader.* Springer Publishing.

Wakeman, C. '3 Steps to Stop Venting Among Your Co-Workers'. LinkedIn.

Wakeman, C. 'These are the three sources of drama'. LinkedIn.

https://jokojokes.com/leadership-jokes.html.

Sherman, R. O. *The Nurse Leader Coach: Become the boss no one wants to leave.* 2019.

Bungay Stainer, M. *The Coaching Habit: Say less, ask more and change the way you lead.* 2016.

Moss Canter, R. Rosabeth Moss Kanter Quotes. BrainyQuote.

Johnson, M, Suskewicz, J. 2020. *Lead From the Future: How to turn visionary thinking into breakthrough growth.* Harvard Business Review press.

Armstrong, H. (2007). 'Hestia and Coaching: Speaking the "hearth" of the matter'. *International Journal of Evidence Based Coaching and Mentoring*, 30-39.

CHAPTER 8

Goleman, D., Boyatzis, R. Mckee, A. *The New Leaders: Transforming the art of leadership into the science of results.* 2002. Timewarner paperbacks.

Quote by Charles Darwin: 'It is not the strongest of the species that sur … ' (goodreads.com).

James I. A. 'The Rightful Demise of the Sh*t Sandwich: Providing Effective Feedback'. (2015). *Behavioural and Cognitive Psychotherapy*, 43(6), 759–766. https://doi.org/10.1017/S1352465814000113.

Jackson, P. Z. McKergow, M. *The Solutions Focus: Making coaching and change simple.* 2007. Nicholas Brealey International.

Goldsmith, M. 2007. Feed Forward.

Seligman, M. Railton, P., Baumeister, R.F., Sripada, C. *Homo Prospectus.* 2022. Oxford University press.

British Hypnosis Research and Training Institute. 'What is Ericksonian Hypnosis? Definition & History'. BHRTI (britishhypnosisresearch.com).

Yapko, M.D. *Trancework: An introduction to the practice of clinical hypnosis.* 4th edition. 2012. Routledge.

Grenny, J., Patterson, K., McMillan, R. Switzler, AL, Gregory, E. *Crucial Conversations: Tools for talking when stakes are high.* 3rd edition. 2022. McGraw Hill books.

SARA model.

Dweck, C. Mindset: *The new psychology of success.* 1st edition. (2006).

Cy Wakeman, TEDX talk. 'Ditch the Drama – How to Live Happy in a Messy World'. YouTube.

CHAPTER 9

Sir Dave Brailsford. 'CORE Principle and Marginal Gains'. YouTube.

Clear, J. 'This Coach Improved Every Tiny Thing By 1% And Here's What Happened'.(jamesclear.com).

Bungay Stainer, M. *The Coaching Habit: Say less, ask more and change the way you lead.* Page two.

Blanchard. K. H. Quote by Ken Blanchard : 'There is a difference between interest and comm … ' (goodreads.com)

Seligman, M. Railton, P., Baumeister, R.F., Sripada, C. *Homo Prospectus.* 2022. Oxford University press.

Dispenza, J. *Breaking the Habit of Being Yourself.* (2012). Hay House.

Walking Meditation Collection – Unlimited with Dr Joe Dispenza.

The Kylego Exercise – Kyle Cease.

'Gandhi Didn't Actually Ever Say, "Be the Change You Want to See in the World." Here's the Real Quote … ' Christian Soschner. Medium.

Rock, D. 'Managing with the Brain in Mind by David Rock'. Academia.edu.

Griffin, M., & Clark, C. M. (2014). 'Revisiting Cognitive Rehearsal as an Intervention Against Incivility and Lateral Violence in Nursing: 10 years later'. *Journal of Continuing Education in Nursing*, 45(12), 535–544. https://doi.org/10.3928/00220124-20141122-02

Herman, T. *The Alter Ego Effect: The power of secret identities to transform your life.* (2019). Harper Business.

Why Introverts Learn Faster. Harvard business school research. (thenextweb.com).

McCashen, W. 'The strength approach: A strengths-based resource for sharing power and creating change'. (2005). St Lukes Innovative resources.

Gollwitzer, P.M., Wieber, F., Myers, A. L., McCrea, S.M., (2009) first published in: 'Then a Miracle Occurs: focusing on behaviour in social psychological theory and research'. Purdue Symposium on Psychological services. Christopher R. Agnew (ed). Oxford University Press, pp. 137-167. How to maximize implementation intention effects (uni-konstanz.de).

Robertson, R. *Leading on the Edge: Extraordinary stories and leadership insights from the world's most extreme workplace.* Wiley.

Gibbs reflective cycle Gibbs' Reflective Cycle. The University of Edinburgh.

Borton's Model of Reflection in Nursing. Bartleby.

Sunshine Coast University Hospital. 'How Reflection and Critical Thinking Can Help Avoid Staff Burnout'. Queensland Health.

Dawber, C. O'Brien, T. (2013). 'A Longitudinal, Comparative Evaluation of Reflective Practice Groups of Nurses Working in Intensive Care and Oncology'. *J Nus care*, 3:1 DOI: 10.4172/2167-1168.1000138.

CONCLUSION

Williamson, M. *A Return to Love: Reflections on the principles of A course in miracles.* (1975).

www.ingramcontent.com/pod-product-compliance
Lightning Source LLC
Chambersburg PA
CBHW062129020426
42335CB00013B/1151